Joy for the World

JOY FOR THE WORLD

A Buddhist Play by Candragomin

Translated with an Introduction
and Notes by Michael Hahn

Yeshe De Project

Dharma Publishing

TIBETAN TRANSLATION SERIES

Buddha's Lions
Calm and Clear
Elegant Sayings
The Fortunate Aeon
Golden Zephyr
Joy for the World
Kindly Bent to Ease Us
Legend of the Great Stupa
Life and Liberation of Padmasambhava
The Marvelous Companion
Master of Wisdom
Mind in Buddhist Psychology
Mother of Knowledge
The Voice of the Buddha

This book is produced in cooperation with the Yeshe De Buddhist Research and Translation Project. Founded in 1983, the Yeshe De Project draws its inspiration from Ye-shes-sde, a direct disciple of Padmasambhava, whose works establish him as a translator without parallel in the history of Dharma transmission.

Thanka courtesy of the St. Louis Art Museum.
Purchase: W. K. Bixby Fund

Library of Congress Cataloging-in-Publication Data
Candragomin.
Joy for the world.
(Tibetan translation series)
Translation of: Lokānandananāṭaka.
1. Gautama Buddha – Pre-existence – Drama.
I. Hahn, Michael. II. Title. III. Series.
PK3794.C352L613 1987 895'42 87-22257
ISBN 0-89800-148-X

Typeset in Mergenthaler Goudy Old Style.
Printed and bound in the United States of America by Dharma Press.

9 8 7 6 5 4 3 2 1

Publisher's Preface

Candragomin, the author of the Lokānanda, is revered as one of the greatest of all Buddhist teachers. According to the account by the historian Tāranātha, he was recognized as a child prodigy at the age of seven, when he defeated a noted philosopher in debate. He quickly acquired skill in all fields of knowledge, and, though his works on grammar gained special fame, he is renowned as well for his devotion and his spiritual attainments.

As he grew to manhood, Candragomin devoted himself to the worship of both Tārā and Avalokiteśvara and taught the Mahāyāna extensively. In his later life, he turned from the study of worldly subjects to devote himself exclusively to the Dharma. Unlike most of the famous Buddhist masters of his age, he never became a monk.

In *Joy for the World*, Candragomin makes use of his literary skills to present a dramatic account of the Buddha in a past life as the Prince Maṇicūḍa, who fulfilled through his perfect generosity the highest standards of moral conduct. On a first reading of the play, the beauty of Candragomin's imagery and his delightful use of humor stand out. The Bodhisattva and those around him are presented in all their humanity, making this work particularly accessible to a Western audience accustomed to psychological characterizations in literature.

On rereading, however, the real substance of the play comes to the fore. The nobility of the hero becomes increasingly evident, and elements of the plot that had first seemed exaggerated take on new meaning. The play can become a powerful teaching, inspiring and evocative. At the same time, it remains a thoroughly enjoyable work that stimulates the imagination and offers rich aesthetic delight: a classic of Sanskrit and world literature.

Buddhist drama is little known in the West, and Dharma Publishing is grateful to have the opportunity to present this expression of the Buddhist teachings to the English-speaking world. We are especially grateful to Professor Hahn for his work on this translation, which succeeds to a remarkable extent in communicating the beauty of the original text. Professor Hahn's enthusiasm for the drama is evident throughout, and the reader will benefit from the care and appreciation with which he has carried out the task of translation.

Dedicated to all who look to the Dharma
for guidance and inspiration.

Acknowledgement

In preparing the present work, I relied on the original Tibetan, the extant Sanskrit verses, and my own previous German translation, published in the series *Asiatische Forschungen* (which also contains the usual scholarly apparatus and a detailed analysis). The English translation was prepared in Kathmandu, Nepal, where I worked on it together with my good friend Bill Templer. The translation has also benefited from the careful editorial assistance of the staff of Dharma Publishing.

M. H.

Introduction

During the first five centuries of its existence, from the beginning of the fifth century B.C. until the end of the first century A.D., Buddhism amassed a huge corpus of canonical scriptures. These texts were considered to be the authentic word of the Buddha himself: his sermons, known as Sūtras; the rules and regulations of the monastic order, or Vinaya; and systematically arranged lists of the basic tenets of Buddhist philosophy, known as Abhidharma. These three kinds of teachings became known as the Tripiṭaka, or "triple basket." The Tripiṭaka forms the nucleus of all the later writings of Indian Buddhism.

With its emphasis on monastic discipline and renunciation, the Tripiṭaka might seem an unlikely source of poetry, let alone drama. Yet the Buddhism of India, whether it be considered a religion or a philosophy, numbered among its followers a galaxy of the finest poets of their age. These writers, inspired by the Buddha's teachings, contributed in essential ways to the transformation of Sanskrit, helping to make this ancient classical language into one of the most refined media of world literature. The greatest among them blended form and content in unique ways, leaving a legacy that we can readily appreciate today.

Several elements of poetry can be found within the Tripiṭaka itself; for example, alliteration, paronomasy, figura etymologica, parallelism, concatenation, and so forth. In addition, numerous stories offer dramatic accounts of the Buddha and his disciples in this life or in previous existences.

It remains as an open question, however, whether these poetic devices were employed for aesthetic reasons. There are good grounds for believing that they belong to the stock of well-developed techniques already current in India at the time of the Buddha for memorizing large quantities of orally transmitted texts in the shortest possible time. These rhetorical techniques would quite naturally have been employed by the Buddha and his followers. To point this out does not deny the poetic quality of many of the Sūtras and other texts of the Tripiṭaka, but does suggest that these elements played the role of a fine but casual accessory to the content.

The main goal of Buddhism could be described as freeing human beings from the bonds of existence. Hence, many of the teachings try to reduce and eventually annihilate those feelings and emotions that strengthen attachment to this world. Nonetheless, it was perhaps only inevitable that converts to Buddhism would find ways to express their love and enthusiasm for the new religion and its founder. The oldest testimony of these feelings are the Theragāthās and Therīgāthās, "The Verses of the Elders" and "The Verses of the Nuns." Recently it has been shown that quite a few of these stanzas are lightly disguised transformations of secular poetry of the time, such as love songs and descriptions of nature, which were obviously much in vogue. For example, Theragāthā 51, attributed to Godhika, rings with a simple joy:

> It rains like good singing.
> My hut is thatched and pleasant,
> My mind is well-concentrated:
> So let it rain if it likes.

The following stanzas (Theragāthā 1068–1071), attributed to Mahākassapa, are more ornate:

Clothed in umma flowers,
like the sky covered with clouds;
strewn with varied flocks of birds,
those crags delight me.

Not full of worldly people,
but sought out by herds of wild animals,
strewn with varied flocks of birds,
those crags delight me.

With clear waters and broad rocks,
full of yaks,
their pools covered with sevala weed,
those crags delight me.

I do not get such pleasure
from the five kinds of musical instruments,
as when with concentrated mind
I gain insight rightly into the Dharma.

The real encounter of Buddhism and poetry, however, took place at the beginning of the first century A.D., or perhaps somewhat earlier. By this time the Buddhist Dharma had established itself so firmly and gained such persuasive force in ethics and philosophy that quite a few educated Brahmins converted. They brought with them the vast store of Brahmanical learning, including both sciences and arts, not to mention the huge mine of popular and higher Hindu mythology.

Not only in Buddhism, but in all of Indian literature, we find that at this time the various genres suddenly present themselves in almost full-fledged form. Although it seems that great progress must have been made in the preceding centuries, very little from the earlier period has survived. We can only guess how and in what milieu the earliest surviving texts came into being.

One fact, however, is quite clear: The earliest specimens of the various types of ornate literature stem from Buddhist authors. We cannot say whether it was Buddhist authors who developed these forms, or whether these authors simply brought them to such a degree of perfection that earlier works were consigned to oblivion. In either case, the contribution of Buddhist authors was decisive.

Among Buddhist writers of the first rank using Sanskrit as their medium of expression were Aśvaghoṣa in the first century A.D., followed by Mātṛceṭa, Nāgārjuna, Kumāralāta, Haribhaṭṭa, and (in the fifth century) the author of the present work, the Buddhist master Candragomin. Unfortunately, much of their work survives only in Tibetan or Chinese translations or in fragmentary or mutilated form. How much of the literary production of this era has been irretrievably lost is a matter for speculation.

Aśvaghoṣa, the first of these authors (identified in Tibetan sources with Mātṛceṭa) is the author of two long epic poems, one based on the life of the Buddha and another on the humorous story of the Buddha's half-brother Nanda. In addition, Aśvaghoṣa is the author of the oldest known Sanskrit dramas, of which only fragments survive.

Similar themes are found in later narrative works. The Jātakamālā of Āryaśūra, in particular, is the unsurpassed masterpiece of Buddhist narrative style. Well-known accounts of the Buddha's past lives are presented in a highly accomplished ornate style, enriched by countless well-turned moral maxims and beautiful descriptions of nature. Āryaśūra's successor, Haribhaṭṭa, also wrote a Jātakamālā, characterized by a greater flexibility and smoothness of language and a remarkable independence with regard to the arrangement of subject matter. It is against this background that we can place the Lokānanda of Candragomin.

Regarding Candragomin himself, considerable scholarly research and controversy seem to have left the following facts clear: Candragomin is the author of both the Lokānanda and the famous Śiśyalekha, or "Letter to a Disciple," a poetic introduction to Buddhist teachings. He also gained fame among Sanskrit grammarians as the founder of the so-called Cāndra system of Sanskrit grammar. As for his dates, the reliable evidence, including stylistic criteria, all points to the fifth century A.D. The statement by the seventh century pilgrim I-Tsing that Candragomin was his contemporary has made for some confusion on this score, but it seems necessary on the basis of the record as a whole to conclude that I-Tsing was simply misinformed or misunderstood his sources.

Like the Jātakamālā and many other Buddhist literary works, the Lokānanda is based on a well-known account of the Buddha in a past life as a Bodhisattva. Generosity such as that exhibited by Prince Maṇicūḍa is a theme quite familiar in the Jātaka tales, and the specific story of Prince Maṇicūḍa can be found in several different versions in the surviving Buddhist literature. However, though the material was well-known, Candragomin gives it a special life and vigor in adapting it to the conventions of Sanskrit drama.

For those who wish to see the difference between the source materials from which Candragomin drew his story and his adaption of this legend for the stage, here is a summary of the Maṇicūḍa story in its oldest known form.

In the city of Sāketa, the present city of Oudh, live king Brahmadatta and his wife, queen Kāntimatī, who conceives a child. Her pregnancy produces in her the wish to perform numerous meritorious acts, including the giving of gifts, food, and medical care to the needy and delivering a sermon. Under wondrous circumstances a son with a miraculous crest jewel (cūḍāmaṇi) is born. Due to this auspicious sign, he is named Maṇicūḍa, meaning "he who bears a jewel on his crest."

Having become king himself, Maṇicūḍa has alms halls erected and admonishes the people to lead a moral life. In a very short remark it is mentioned that a sage by the name of Bhavabhūti, living in the Himālaya, finds a girl in a lotus pond, brings her up under the name of Padmāvatī and offers her as wife to King Maṇicūḍa. He asks as reward that, on the occasion of the presentation of his spouse Padmāvatī, the king perform a sacrifice and dedicate the merit resulting from it to the sage. Maṇicūḍa agrees, marries Padmāvatī, and after some time a son, Padmottara, is born to them.

One day Maṇicūḍa preaches a sermon to the people at which the four guardians of the world rejoice to such a degree that they decide to help Maṇicūḍa to become enlightened. He then performs the sacrifice of "unrestrained" giving for the benefit of Bhavabhūti to which the neighboring king Duṣprasaha is invited. At the ceremony, a demon (rākṣasa) appears and demands food. As he insists on having fresh flesh, Maṇicūḍa, despite the general dismay, offers himself. The demon devours him almost completely before he discloses himself as Indra in disguise. King Maṇicūḍa's body is thereupon restored by an "act of truth" (satyakriyā). Indra begs pardon for his trial. Then Maṇicūḍa generously distributes further gifts and dedicates the merit to Bhavabhūti.

The great sage Vāhika then enters and demands the wife and child of Maṇicūḍa as a reward for his teacher Marīci. Maṇicūḍa complies with this request too and bids farewell to Padmāvatī and Padmottara. When King Duṣprasaha demands the royal elephant Bhadragiri, which had already been given to the priest Brahmaratha, a war breaks out and Sāketa is besieged. Maṇicūḍa has himself left for the Himālaya in order to buy back Bhadragiri. There he lives the life of a hermit, engaging in moral and philosophical reflections. In the meantime, the minister Subāhu defeats Duṣprasaha and redeems Padmottara from Marīci.

Indra decides to test Maṇicūḍa again. He sends the devaputra Dharma who, disguised as a hunter, takes Padmāvatī by force from Marīci's hermitage. Maṇicūḍa hears her cries and rescues her. Māra, disguised as a young man, tries to persuade Maṇicūḍa to return to Sāketa with Padmāvatī but Maṇicūḍa instead sends her back to Marīci, who releases her and magically transports her to Sāketa by air.

In Duṣprasaha's kingdom plague has broken out. He sends five Brāhmins to Maṇicūḍa to request his miraculous crest jewel because of its healing power. Maṇicūḍa gives it to them, though his skull must be cleft for the jewel to be removed. By the natural phenomena accompanying this event, the chief personages of the narration are all alerted, and gather at Maṇicūḍa's side. He stresses that he does not regret anything and does not feel any hatred against anybody. By this "act of truth" he is cured once again, returns to Sāketa, and lives there happily as king with his family. Duṣprasaha, in whose kingdom plague has disappeared, begs his pardon.

There are remnants of a second version of the legend, which is longer and perhaps also older than the one just summarized. Its difference consists in a detailed description of the period from Maṇicūḍa's birth to his succession to the throne and his marriage. This is the version Candragomin seems to have relied upon for Acts One through Three of his drama. What follows is an outline of the content of this additional portion.

As a young man Maṇicūḍa retires to the solitude of the forest and reflects on renouncing worldly life. During this time Padmāvatī is declared Maṇicūḍa's bride without his knowing it. This is done through the intervention of Padmāvatī's friend Ratnāvalī, who is a vidyādharī, or heavenly fairy. She takes a portrait of Maṇicūḍa to the hermitage, whereupon Padmāvatī falls in love with him. Later on Ratnāvalī shows a picture of Padmāvatī to Kāntimatī, Maṇicūḍa's mother, who acknowledges her as an appropriate daughter-in-law. When the wedding cord is taken to Maṇicūḍa he at first refuses to return to worldly life. Only the threat by Padmāvatī's friends that they will commit suicide makes him change his mind. At that point the marriage and the succession to the throne take place, as in the other version.

At the time that Candragomin wrote, the drama of India had at least five centuries of tradition behind it, and its basic forms were well-established. This dramatic tradition (of which the Lokānanda is one of the oldest surviving examples) is the only known parallel to the classical drama of Greece and Rome. It is characterized by its formal structure, which consists of a prologue (an essential element), several acts (usually from four to ten, although there are also one-act plays), frequent interludes that represent breaks in the action, and a conclusion.

The subject matter for such dramas could be well-known tales or stories based on the author's own invention. In either case, they had to be adapted in such a way that they fulfilled a large number of requirements. There were strict rules for the nature and development of the plot, and a prescribed set of emotions that had to be part of the action. Various scenes and events could not be shown on the stage but had to be described or referred to in the interludes. A fixed set of characters was required; for example, the jester or friend of the hero, the friends of the heroine, the heroine's maid-servants, holy personages, and so forth. Numerous other formal elements were required as well.

A striking peculiarity of the Indian drama, which is not really reflected in the present translation, is the use of different languages by different characters. Sanskrit, the language of the educated, is usually spoken by men (with the jester a noteworthy exception) and a few high-ranking women. Actors from the lower classes and the uneducated use various vernacular languages, referred to collectively as Prākrit. The language of the characters is a mix of prose and verses. The stanzas were usually sung, with many repetitions and accompanied by musical instruments. Thus, the total effect resembled that of a Western opera or musical.

The audience for such a play knew and respected all the conventions of the form. They expected from the author that he show his skill in handling these formal requirements, creating an ideal blend of a well-structured story told in elegant language and dramatic form, mixing moral and ethical teachings with beautiful verses and songs, dances, and the extensive use of humor. Although only eleven verses of the Lokānanda survive in Sanskrit, and the Tibetan translation is less than perfect, there seems to be every reason to believe that the Lokānanda would have been judged as meeting these standards at the highest level.

The popularity the Lokānanda enjoyed more than two hundred years after it had been composed is attested to by a statement of the Chinese pilgrim I-Tsing who writes in his record on his visit to India:

> The great scholar Yue-Kuan ['moon-official'; that is, Candragomin], from the East of India, composed poetry about the crown prince p'i-shu-an-ta-lo [= Viśvāntara, erroneously for Maṇicūḍa], hitherto known as Su-ta-na, and all people sing and dance [i.e., stage] it throughout the five countries of India.

With the Sanskrit original of the play lost we can no longer fully appreciate the skill with which Candragomin had handled the Sanskrit language as well as the various middle-indic vernaculars in his play, a skill of which his beautiful poem "Letter to the Disciple" gives us an authentic impression. However, the content and spirit of his play can still be felt quite strongly, even after its migration from Sanskrit to Tibetan, Tibetan to German, and German to English. The message of the play is so humanitarian and universal that its appeal can be readily felt by modern readers, despite the fact that they live in a civilization immeasurably different from that of Candragomin's time.

We owe a great debt to the Indian pandit Kīrticandra and the Tibetan monk Tragpa Gyeltsen (Grags-pa-rgyal-mtshan), who six and a half centuries ago translated the Lokānanda from Sanskrit into Tibetan in Kathmandu, Nepal, thereby preserving at least one Buddhist dramatic work in its entirety. It is only through their efforts that we can enjoy today what the people of India cherished for almost a millenium.

A Note on the Translation

Contrary to the impression the reader might get from the English rendering of the Lokānanda as presented in this book, the translation of Candragomin's play has not been a simple or straightforward task. As documented in detail in my scholarly publications on the Lokānanda, it is almost certain that several factors negatively influenced Candragomin's original text in the course of translation and further transmission. The manuscript used by the two translators was obviously difficult to read or even faulty in several places. To give only one example: in IV.23d we find the expression *lhag pa'i ska rags* "(having) an excessive girdle." In Sanskrit this would be **adhi-mekhalā*. This stanza introduces the Goddess of Earth, one of whose most common epithets is "girded by the ocean." By simply adding one letter we can change *adhi-mekhalā* to *abdhi-mekhalā*, and this is exactly what we would expect, because *abdhi* means "ocean." Therefore, we can safely assume that in this place the Sanskrit manuscript (which is now lost) contained a mistake or that it was misread by the translators.

There are many more instances of this kind, some of them much more difficult to recognize and to solve. The clue for the solution of these passages is not so much a good knowledge of Tibetan, but a familiarity with the Indian drama and the stylistic peculiarities of the Sanskrit of the 5th century A.D. Moreover, it could be shown that in several places an originally correct translation was distorted in the course of transmission, or that the translator used an orthography different from what later became the standard of Classical Tibetan. In all these places a literal translation of the Tibetan text as contained in the bsTan-'gyur would not have yielded what Candragomin had in mind when he wrote his play and also not what the two translators intended to express in Tibetan.

As it has been the main objective to restore the words and meaning of the original play as faithfully as possible, all the results of textual and literary criticism have been incorporated in the present English translation. Moreover, some difficult expressions which are not easily intelligible for non-Indians and would therefore have required explanation in a footnote are accompanied by a kind of commentary or paraphrase; for example, "the 'Bearer of Treasures', the earth", where "the earth" is added by the translator. And finally, at those ten or twenty places where even now the exact meaning of a certain word or passage is not fully clear, the most likely solution has been selected without entering into a detailed philological discussion of possible alternatives.

The original plan to print the English translation of the Lokānanda along with the original Tibetan text of the play has been abandoned because of the very difficulties outlined above. The inclusion of the Tibetan would have required another 100 pages of detailed notes and a glossary to enable the reader to understand in each case why it has been translated in such and such way. We feel that this would necessarily have distracted most of the readers from the central part of the book, the beauty and depth of a truly Buddhist drama.

Dramatis Personae

Male:

The stage director

The hero Maṇicūḍa, first prince, later king in Śāketa

*King Brahmadatta, father of Maṇicūḍa

Padmottara, son of Maṇicūḍa and Padmavātī

The jester Gautama, a Brāhman and friend of Maṇicūḍa

Subāhu, prime-minister under king Maṇicūḍa

The royal sacrificial priest

Mauñja, a Brāhman

*Mañjula, one of the servants of king Maṇicūḍa

*King Duṣprasaha, an enemy of king Maṇicūḍa

A Brāhman, sent to Maṇicūḍa by Duṣprasaha

The hermit Bhavabhūti, foster-father of Padmavātī

His pupil

The ascetic Marīci

The God Indra, first in the guise of a demon

Two Śabaras, wild tribal forest dwellers

A servant

A male heavenly fairy

Retinue of the palace

Voices from the dressing-room behind the stage

Female:

The dancer, wife of the stage director

The heroine Padmavātī, foster-daughter of the hermit

*Queen Kāntimatī, mother of Maṇicūḍa

The heavenly fairy Ratnāvalī, a friend of Padmavātī

Mādhavī, a friend of Padmavātī

Bindumatī, a friend of Padmavātī

Parṇikā, one of Padmavātī's maid-servants

Kuntalikā, one of Padmavātī's maid-servants

A maid-servant

A heavenly fairy

The goddess of the earth

*Does not appear onstage.

Approximate pronunciation: "c" is pronounced like ch, "ṣ" and "ś" are pronounced like sh. Other diacriticals have a more subtle effect.

Lokānandanāṭaka

'Jig rten kun tu dga' ba'i zlos gar

Homage to the Omniscient One!

ACT ONE

Prelude

Benediction

1 With this handful of flowers I venerate
the feet of the Jina, Buddha, the Victorious One:
flowers now permeated through and through
by rich quantities of fine pollen
from blossoms juicy and budding,
after the swarming garland of bees,
buzzing indistinctly, have with their myriad feet
set these leaves to trembling;
flowers full and heavy with great globules of nectar.
May He accordingly grant you all
tranquility of mind!

Moreover:

2 "O you whose loving character is vast
beyond all measure, you who were once so blissfully
embraced by your wife Yaśodharā —
in your great compassion should you not also show
toward us a similar equanimity?
But we of course must not behave as did
the noble mistress Yaśodharā!"

O, may you gain knowledge of the Buddha
who was so addressed by the envy-drunk daughters of
Māra, the god of desire!

3 The hosts of Māra emit an ear-shattering howl
as our guide, the Buddha, sends them
scattering pell-mell in wild flight
and they are trod upon
and trampled down under Māra's feet.
Māra, angered and enraged
by the Buddha's most perfect Enlightenment
has now pulled and pointed his bow at Him.
The love-maddened daughters
of Anaṅga (Māra) shed tears,
while the immortal ones
rejoice to see this scene.
May the invincible goddess Aparājitā,
who accompanies the Buddha
endowed with the Ten Powers,
protect and watch over you!

Prologue

Enter the stage director at the close of the benediction.

STAGE DIRECTOR:

4 The poet Candradāsa (Candragomin) has composed
a completely new kind of play:
the drama *Joy for the World.*
Therefore I will now present it
to the audience here assembled.

Candragomin is certainly a poet

5 Who, in answer to a wish
directed to the goddess Tārā, was born
into the race of Jātukarṇa in the east of India,
and who achieved great fame
as her son and follower,
though he was unable to bear
the burden of rule;

and who moreover

6 has so mastered the most magnificent means
of verbal ornament and expression
that his compositions in verse and prose,
these spacious bathing places of the learned,
are not in the least limited

to the mere description of a sole and single theme;
a poet who has also written a grammar of Sanskrit,
concise, abundantly clear
yet comprehensive in scope,
and has destroyed the great welter
of worldly passions and earthbound ignorance.

At the sound of the musical instruments marking the beginning of the prelude, he calls his wife onstage.

STAGE DIRECTOR: Hello there, my wife! Come over here!

His wife, the dancer, enters, stricken with grief.

DANCER: My husband, here I stand! Command me your will!

STAGE DIRECTOR: My wife, why are you so aggrieved?

DANCER: Why shouldn't I feel grief,

7 when our only son, a boy who
on the strength of your good name alone
is able to assume a high position
in the world of men, declares:
"I shall most definitely enter the Buddhist order;
I will see to it that my present life
becomes fruitful"?

STAGE DIRECTOR: After all, he's not a Bodhisattva, is he?

DANCER: My husband! "Were he not a Bodhisattva, then nothing would have descended from the heavens at his birth, nor would anything have blossomed forth upon the wishing-tree of paradise." These are my thoughts. Moreover, I call that man a Bodhisattva who in his compassion takes delight in living for the salvation of all mankind.

STAGE DIRECTOR: My wife, the matter is like this:

8 In a Bodhisattva, the tender shoot
of the aspiration for supreme enlightenment,
which has sprouted forth
from the seed of compassion,
grows ever upward, and the buds of moral perfection
unfold like desired objects upon the wishing-tree.

But come now, we've had enough of this grief and grieving! By dint of his great merit he will attain the highest happiness and bliss. Begin now with your song!

DANCER: My husband, referring to what season of the year should I begin my song?

STAGE DIRECTOR: My wife, sing now of the season of flowers, in which everything springs forth and blossoms anew, and all is permeated by the fragrance of the buds of the mango tree, a season in which we pluck flowers and the swarms of bees frolic joyously!

DANCER: Such is the nature of springtime:

9 The sun rises anew and breathes fresh life
into the lotus blossoms, ravaged by hoar-frost,
while the mild southerly breezes in like manner
cheer and delight mankind.
From every point of the compass
the blossoms of the palāśa tree

gleam blood-red like meat quartered and minced,
and the cool-rayed glowing orb of the moon
is fastened to the heavens
like a *crest-jewel* (cūḍāmaṇi),
in its radiance against the sky.

Voices from the dressing-room backstage:

Exceedingly wonderful! Quite wonderful!

STAGE DIRECTOR (*listening carefully*): What's that? (*He looks closely, then says in recognition*):

10 After the heavenly fairy, the Vidyādharī,
has caught sight of the Prince *Maṇicūḍa*,
named for the crest-jewel upon his head,
her hairs stand on end and she trembles in her joy,
while the lotuses of her hands
dance back and forth,
and her anklets swing,
touching the hem of her garment.
She rushes away into the heavens,
to the peak of Mt. Himavant.

But now, in accordance with the wishes of the audience, we shall present a complete performance of the play.

The two exit from the stage.

End of the Prelude

The Vidyādharī or heavenly fairy Ratnāvalī comes onstage and dances about, after having recited the following verse:

RATNĀVALĪ: Wonderful! So wonderful!

11 Even the gods seldom behold
such a human being here on earth.
I am overcome by a deep joy.
Shall I approach my dear friend
and companion Padmāvatī
and pass on to her the weight I carry?

Without giving any further thought to why she has come and why she is here, she reaches the hermitage where her dear friend lives and enters there, bedazzled.

Here comes my dear friend Padmāvatī now, accompanied by Mādhavī and engrossed in conversation with her. They walk upon a path strewn with nāgakesara blossoms, on flagstones covered by plentiful pollen from flowers in full bloom, the bounteous burden of bees' feet!

Mādhavī and Padmāvatī appear onstage.

PADMĀVATĪ: O Mādhavī, I believe my heart is drunk with rapture. (*She sees her dear friend Ratnāvalī, the Vidyādharī.*) Why haven't you joined us yet?

RATNĀVALĪ (*listening carefully*): O Padmāvatī, do not fall prey to confusion through what I now must tell you!

PADMĀVATĪ and MĀDHAVĪ (*exclaiming*): O joy! O joy! (*Seized by excitement the two rush forward toward the Vidyādharī.*) Tell us! What's happened, what's happened?

RATNĀVALĪ: I have beheld something that is worthy of being seen by all beings blessed with sight; through this I have reaped the true fruits of my vision.

PADMĀVATĪ and MĀDHAVĪ: What have you seen? Tell us!

The Vidyādharī once more repeats her words. The two repeat their question, and the Vidyādharī embraces Padmāvatī.

RATNĀVALĪ: I am overcome by deep joy! Only if I could rival Sarasvatī, the goddess of speech, in my eloquence, could I fully express what I feel.

PADMĀVATĪ and MĀDHAVĪ: Your joy seems almost to be something extraordinarily weighty and crushing.

RATNĀVALĪ: When your eyes behold him you experience supreme joy, even if you may have seen others exceedingly attractive before.

PADMĀVATĪ and MĀDHAVĪ: Silly goose — are you finished now with your affectations? Let us share in your joy as well!

RATNĀVALĪ:

12 The one my eyes have now beheld,
whose fire has been mastered,
who projects without surcease
the splendor of his power,
in appearance gleaming and majestic,
delights the eyes of all those well-versed
in the moral commandments (astrological laws)

of the four directions of the compass,
and in the multitude of all artistic skills
(the 16 phases of the moon).

PADMĀVATĪ and MĀDHAVĪ: My dear, do you perhaps mean the moon?

RATNĀVALĪ (*indignantly*): The person I mean — and I certainly haven't described him as if he were the moon — is outstanding in a very special way. As to the moon, its dark spots resemble the gazelle. Is that the case with him?

PADMĀVATĪ and MĀDHAVĪ: Or is it then Madana, the God of Love, whom you mean?

RATNĀVALĪ: Has Madana, who hums his *hmm* and is like a moth above the tongues of flame, who (his body having been consumed by fire) has lost all corporal existence, — ever appeared as one radiant and gleaming, whose energy has been mastered?

PADMĀVATĪ and MĀDHAVĪ: Then tell us what you mean!

RATNĀVALĪ: I will tell you, so listen well! Since I had learned from the conversations of the Vidyādharīs that "Prince Maṇicūḍa has such and such a nature," I journeyed, full of great joy and boundless curiosity, from here to the city of Sāketa. It was there I laid eyes upon the son to whom Kāntimatī, the consort of the king Brahmadatta, had given birth. None can compare to him! He is distinguished by supreme physical beauty and the promise of great happiness. Profound is his compassion; he gives to each and every person whatsoever that person desires. His name is Prince Maṇicūḍa. To behold him is to attain the ideal of perfection longed for by all. After a likeness of his body and external appearance had been painted on a canvas for the daughter of some king or another, it was stolen during transport and carried off by Vidyādharīs.

PADMĀVATĪ and MĀDHAVĪ (*with growing longing and desire*): Go on! Where is it now?

RATNĀVALĪ: On this very "Bearer of Treasures," the planet earth!

PADMĀVATĪ and MĀDHAVĪ: O Vidyādharī, you are a "planetary wanderer through the heavens," and have therefore succeeded in seeing him. You have attained perfect satisfaction of your longing to see him, which robbed you so totally of your mind!

RATNĀVALĪ: Not so hastily! Your longing too will soon be satisfied.

MĀDHAVĪ: Why should someone grant us this happy fate?

RATNĀVALĪ: He has, however, one imperfection!

PADMĀVATĪ and MĀDHAVĪ: What sort of imperfection? Tell us!

RATNĀVALĪ: That he shirks his duties as father of a family.

MĀDHAVĪ and PADMĀVATĪ: Well, a wishing jewel — one that fulfills *all* desires — is a rare thing in this world!

RATNĀVALĪ: Your mention of the wishing jewel reminds me of something else about him, something marvelous beyond compare: the crest-jewel which he has worn like a wishing jewel upon his head since birth.

MĀDHAVĪ: Wonderful!

RATNĀVALĪ: But what is so wonderful about him? Standing here, have you ever seen that one so far away, across all this distance?

MĀDHAVĪ: But did we ever have a chance to see him?

RATNĀVALĪ: No — but I have brought him along!

MĀDHAVĪ and PADMĀVATĪ (*looking about in all directions in embarrassed excitement*): Where? O where is he then?

From her upper garment, the Vidyādharī takes a portrait painted on canvas and shows it to them. Blushing, they gaze bashfully at the painting, crowding in close to Ratnāvalī on both sides.

Mādhavī and Padmāvatī both speak at once.

PADMĀVATĪ: Your words have given birth in me to a joy that is vain and empty, for it is not based on a real object.

MĀDHAVĪ: Like you, he is of splendid bearing and appearance. Tell me, my dear friend, does he have any imperfection whatsoever?

PADMĀVATĪ (*gazes at length upon the portrait*): He does indeed have one.

RATNĀVALĪ (*indignantly*): What kind of a fault or imperfection? Tell us!

MĀDHAVĪ (*after looking at Padmāvatī*): He is "unspeakable" . . . I mean, it is impossible to speak to him.

RATNĀVALĪ: Padmāvatī, don't be sad. I also painted a portrait of you on canvas and presented it to Queen Kāntimatī. She looked at it, was pleased and said: "Now I have beheld the face of a bride and daughter-in-law. If I gain her as a daughter-in-law, I will be very happy."

PADMĀVATĪ (*angrily*): My dear friend, is it right and proper to mock me so?

MĀDHAVĪ (*filled with great joy*): And what happened after that? Go on!

RATNĀVALĪ: And then King Brahmadatta himself saw the portrait. The two glanced at each other and said: "She matches the prince, our son!" After the two had examined the portrait themselves, they asked a servant to show it to the young man. Whereupon he contemplated the portrait for some time, and then let out a sigh. Well, this was done thanks to the might of the gods!

MĀDHAVĪ: What is his main characteristic?

RATNĀVALĪ: They say he is very much attached to persons deserving veneration and obedience, like parents and ascetics.

Hearing this, Padmāvatī begins to weep.

RATNĀVALĪ (*startled by this, thinks to herself*): Perchance the nectar-like rain of my words has pervaded her through and through with poison! How can she be restored to health again?

Voice from the dressing room offstage, separated by a curtain:

This way!

The three girls think simultaneously to themselves:

Who is coming now?

Enter the sage and his pupil.

THE SAGE BHAVABHŪTI and HIS DISCIPLE:

13 Only she to whom it has been granted
to be the tender mother of a son
and who in her heart knows no sorrow
is a true human being, one who will attain
supreme happiness here on earth.

THE SAGE: My daughter Padmāvatī has been gone quite a long time since she went off to pluck flowers.

14 Has Viṣṇu, perhaps, supposing her to be Lakṣmī,
dragged her off and away by force? Or has the sun,
imagining her face to be
the countenance of the moon,
possessed her through the power
of its irresistible rays?
Or did the Vidyādharīs, after meeting her,
venerate her as Vidyādharī and then abduct her?
Plagued by such thoughts,
my mind raves mad within me,
and I am powerless to make it cease!

DISCIPLE: O my guru, do not surrender yourself to such torments of the heart. None in this world possess the power to violate the teacher's sphere of authority.

The two now walk about the stage. The sage looks in all directions and says sobbing:

SAGE:

15 I am deeply worried and afraid
that she was separated from her companions
while their bodies were hidden
by a veil of swarming bees;
and that subsequently, overtaken by great sorrow,
she stumbled into a well covered over by foliage;
or else that after an intolerable quarrel
with her companions she rushed toward them
overflowing with affection, and tripped and fell;
or that the child is sobbing somewhere all alone.

All three girls see and hear this, and become very excited.

RATNĀVALĪ: Is it her father? What will happen now?

PADMĀVATĪ and MĀDHAVĪ (*in bashful shame*): Father has heard the words we have spoken!

PADMĀVATĪ: Perhaps I will be able to return, unnoticed by father, if I enter this madhūka forest.

After this thought she and Mādhavī enter the forest. The Vidyādharī, in great agitation, approaches the sage and pays him obeisance.

SAGE: May salvation reign supreme! (*Seeing the portrait*) My daughter Ratnāvalī, what is that?

RATNĀVALĪ (*fearfully*): I feel so deeply intimidated that I am unable to speak. Let Father visualize it through meditation!

(*The sage becomes absorbed in meditation. The Vidyādharī is seized by great anxiety.*) What will Father say about this?

SAGE: My daughter, put an end to fear. O, he has quite a goodly bit of strength of character!

Hearing this all three girls are happy once more. They think to themselves:

THE THREE GIRLS: Now we can breathe freely again.

SAGE: Since his childhood they have been telling the tale of his perfect virtues. This man she so desires will make a most excellent mate and an ideal bridegroom.

RATNĀVALĪ: The Exalted One is favorably disposed toward us.

MĀDHAVĪ: O Padmāvatī!

16 An end now to all doubt and doubting:
The goal has been attained!
Most assuredly, the
longing of an ascetic,
a wish which has sprung
from your most heartfelt desire,
will not remain without fruit and consequence.

SAGE: O you, most noble man, who have come into our midst: You merit veneration, even if for now you only appear to our senses in the guise of a picture. (*The Vidyādharī picks flowers and gives them to the sage. The sage presents them as an offering to the painting and contemplates the portrait.*) In truth, it has been painted by a learned artist! For

17 This wondrous painting, in which
the many features of his external appearance:
his stance, expression, bodily proportions and height,
the broad, open surfaces, the minute details
have all been depicted and limned without a flaw,
this portrait whose very eyes appear to move,
seems almost as if it could speak.

Yes, my daughter has truly pinned her heart upon a most delightful object of desire, because

18 This man is of strong character,
and has renounced the pleasures of the senses;
by serving him with full devotion
she will become much like him.

My daughter Ratnāvalī, do you know the whereabouts of your two dear companions?

RATNĀVALĪ: O Exalted One, when they beheld you they went into the forest arbor.

SAGE: Padmāvatī, child, tell me, have you too now learned the ways of shame and modesty? My daughter, Padmāvatī, come over here.

Padmāvatī approaches, trembling with shyness:

SAGE (*looking at Padmāvatī*): Enough of this timidity!

19 You are indeed my pleasure and delight,
you who look upon the world with trusting heart,

with thoughts untainted by doubt; you with a body
unshakable and firm, who stand steadfast
and free from the desire for honor and esteem —
you have the mind of an innocent child.
O you who are by nature beautiful and constant,
why this sense of shame?

Padmāvatī bows down, and the sage touches the crown of her head.

You shall have the man you so fervently desire!

RATNĀVALĪ (*belonging to the family of the sage*): O my dear friend, he is indeed a creator molding the fate of men! Why else should the Exalted One let his voice be heard? I too am greatly pleased by this matter.

DISCIPLE: O guru, make haste! The hour for the Vedic sacrifice has arrived.

SAGE: I see that the appointed time for the midday offering is already upon us. For

20 Even the Vidyādharīs now lie down in leisure
to rest in the shade of the park's trees.
Under their cool and shady canopy
the ruminant beasts rest;
even the water in the trenches dug round the trees
lies still. High above on the mountain peaks
smoke from sacrificial offerings gathers and thickens.

Final Verse

21 Accept now and enjoy
this exceedingly delightful dramatic piece
so rich in originality, a poem
of the noble Candragomin:
a play which treats of a man
august and dispassionate,
a herald of highest religious merit,
who alone and through his world-embracing fame
conquers the universe.

Exit all.

End of Act One

ACT TWO

Entr'acte

Enter Kuntalikā, a maid-servant.

KUNTALIKĀ:

1 This royal race appears to belong
within the world of the gods!
For where else can one find
an event so unparalleled—
should it indeed prove true—
that a bride portrayed but in a painting
is taking part in the bridal ceremony?

She looks around and walks about the stage.

2 The beautiful women
in the villages of the vassal kings
have now adorned themselves so richly
that the village centers are flooded
with the boundless luminosity of the rays
emanating from their jewelry, and seem bedecked
as in a garment of red.

She looks more carefully in a specific direction, and discovering her friend Parṇikā there, she cries out:

KUNTALIKĀ: O Parṇikā, come over here!

The maid-servant acts as though Parṇikā were approaching. Parṇikā steps up to the front of the stage.

PARṆIKĀ: O Kuntalikā, listen! Why do you show such indifference toward the bridal ceremony?

KUNTALIKĀ: O Parṇikā, has not the Prince once again entered the meditation grove, although the Queen has made all arrangements for the bridal ceremony? My thoughts keep returning to this fact.

PARṆIKĀ:

3 Does the Prince ever violate and go against
the word of any person deserving of respect?
Will the rising tide of the ocean
ever wash over its shores?

KUNTALIKĀ: Let the wish of the Queen be his guiding principle!

PARṆIKĀ: Did the Prince leave accompanied by his friend?

KUNTALIKĀ: For just that reason did the Queen say the following words about the undesirable demeanor of the Prince: "Please make sure the honorable Gautama accompanies the Prince; speak therefore to him about this matter. Once you have secured the aid of the honorable Gautama, surely love shall arise in the Prince's heart!"

Parṇikā mimes in dance that this would bring her wish to perfect fulfillment, and then the two express this in mime together.

PARṆIKĀ (*looking off in a specific direction*): O, if this is so, then this is likely the honorable Gautama who now approaches to carry out the order of the most exalted Queen.

KUNTALIKĀ and PARṆIKĀ: Let us now be off to report this to the Queen!

Exit Kuntalikā and Parṇikā.

End of the Entr'acte

Enter the jester or Vidūṣaka Gautama, the friend of the Prince.

GAUTAMA: This now is the message of Queen Kāntimatī for my dear friend, who is taking great pains to live a life undefiled and morally pure by emulating the sages: "Pain dwells within our hearts, for to speak of the bridal ceremony having only seen Padmāvatī's portrait most surely indicates a bride of special suitability." (*He looks up, then continues in thought:*) No matter what I say now to my dear friend, his frame of mind, particularly in this present situation, will of necessity take a corresponding turn and react accordingly. This is of importance, for

4 Even after we have passed to the world beyond,
only when the chain of our family generations
is broken asunder will we reach the final cessation,

like water in the sacrifice
for the departed souls of the dead,
which then ceases its flow.

What words shall we find so that our hearts may think of things more pleasant? (*Looking around, he thinks to himself:*) Here comes Mañjula, the servant of my bosom friend Maṇicūḍa, from the pleasure grove. I'll ask him. (*Aloud*) Hey there, Mañjula, tell me, where is my dear friend? (*Speaking as if to another person*) What is that you say? He's staying in the pleasure grove? Well, I'd better go there then. (*Saying this, he enters the pleasure grove. Looking about, he remarks:*) The flowers, shaken with great vigor in the winds swirled up by the wings of the bees, are enwrapped in the powdery pollen of their stamens, opened wide; they are enveloped by the bees, who circle buzzing above their gaping flowery mouths. (*Not seeing his dear friend, he says:*) According to Mañjula, he should be here. Has he perhaps been carried off by an enchanted Vidyādharī?

Enter the Vidyādharī Ratnāvalī. Filled with sorrow, she thinks to herself:

5 Ever since the moment I described
the Prince's nature and character
to my dear friend Padmāvatī,
she has had a splitting headache.

Her body finds no rest or repose, and the torments piercing her soul are ever on the increase; her companions too are greatly grieved. In this state of mind she shuns her dear friends, and even when they draw near she acts as though they were not present. But I know the heart of the Prince is also torn by terrible torment. (*She glances about, sees the friend of the Prince, and thinks:*) I must see where he's going to now.

GAUTAMA (*glancing about*): Now I will look for my friend upon the pleasure hill, above the artificial fountains whose trembling waves imitate the sound of a waterfall as they plunge down. (*He pantomimes climbing up, and calls out:*) Hey there, hello! (*He spies the Prince on the gigantic jewelled tiles in the grove of Aśoka trees, talking to himself as he walks, and approaches him.*)

RATNĀVALĪ (*thinking to herself*): Now I'll hear what intimate words these two young men are exchanging. (*Approaching him, she sees the emotional state he is in.*)

MAṆICŪḌA (*sighing*): Alas, men crave but for the pleasures of the senses!

6 What form and manner of existence is there
that the soul has not already lived through
in this world a hundred times before?
And what sort of happiness is there
that has not been enjoyed
on countless previous occasions?
What sort of goddesses of happiness are those,
a sweet smile on their lips,
fanned by the moving tails of the yak,
that one has not beheld many a time before?
And yet despite all this,
human desire continues to grow!

GAUTAMA (*having heard this*): May your prosperity increase!

The hero recites the verse once more in a similar melancholy manner.

RATNĀVALĪ (*beating on the drum*): Behold, the water for the souls of the departed dead is being brought for my dear friend.

GAUTAMA: Hello there! Please grant a reply to the good wishes of a Brāhman!

MAṆICŪḌA: Could that be Gautama? How is my good friend? Sit down here next to me!

GAUTAMA (*thinking to himself*): Hearing the words of my friend and properly examining the matter, I note that his melancholy is immense, his mood not at all joyous or glad. Therefore I see as yet no opportunity to speak in a fitting manner about the message of the Queen. I'll say the following words now. (*Aloud*) O my dear friend, look and see!

7 Upon the leaf of a lotus a honey-drunk bee
comes forth from a hole
in the dense network of a devadāru tree,
buzzing her song, and a stream of water
gushes down upon the lotus from above.

RATNĀVALĪ (*thinks to herself*): Splendid, Gautama, splendid! You have compassion for us!

MAṆICŪḌA: Friend, what then do our eyes behold here?

8 All these lotuses,
opened wide, grown to maturity,
and covered with falling pollen,
bear clear testimony to one fact:

how much all beings
in the round of their existence
are subject to impermanence and change.

When the Vidyādharī hears the melancholy of the Prince's words, she is deeply grieved.

GAUTAMA (*thinking to himself*): I'd prefer to speak of other things. (*Aloud*) Fine, something else then.

9 My friend, look and behold the peacocks dancing,
with tails outspread and droplets of water
as necklaces upon their necks.
They watch the torrent of rain
rushing down from the southern water tank
toward the center of the park,
having first savored the taste of honey;
the fountains having been set to sprinkling.

MAṆICŪḌA: Is a fountain then unique in this?

10 The stream of palpable things is likewise ruptured
and cut through in each and every moment,
and all human beings step into this stream
as peacocks into a fountain.

RATNĀVALĪ (*thinking to herself*): I want to clothe my heart in armor and then hear more of this exchange.

GAUTAMA (*reflecting to himself*):

11 Although I have seized upon all the possibilities
by which he might liberate himself
from the hot torments
of the grief which consumes him,
and have unfolded these to him,
each one has caused his grief
to blaze up more fiercely,
like sacrificial butter poured upon the fire.

For this reason I intend to weep here in this desolate forest retreat.

Enter a maid-servant.

MAID-SERVANT (*to herself*): The Queen Kāntimatī has ordered me to bring to the young man the sacramental thread for the bride. And there he is, walking about over yonder. (*She approaches him, bows and does obeisance, then says aloud:*) May the Prince be victorious, may He be victorious! The commandment of the Queen reads: "Tie this sacramental marriage thread, O prudent one, to your own self!"

RATNĀVALĪ (*who cannot bear to hear this, thinks to herself*): Alas, who has been chosen here as a bride?

The Vidūṣaka takes the sacramental marriage thread and places it around the Prince.

MAID-SERVANT (*highly pleased*): O, with this the heartfelt wish of the Queen has been satisfied. (*She walks about the stage and exits.*)

MAṆICŪḌA: My friend, what is the meaning of sending this sacramental thread when there is no occasion that would warrant it?

The Vidūṣaka ponders this silently. When the hero asks him again, he speaks.

GAUTAMA: If my words are not unworthy, I will tell you.

MAṆICŪḌA: Speak, my friend!

GAUTAMA: You are married!

RATNĀVALĪ (*thinks to herself, despairingly*): Alas, how then can he gaze upon the perfect body of my dear friend?

MAṆICŪḌA (*sensing the agitation in their hearts*): What did you say? I'm married?

GAUTAMA: Indeed you are!

MAṆICŪḌA: How has that been accomplished?

GAUTAMA: Ask the sacramental thread!

MAṆICŪḌA: My friend, marriage is an incurable disease, for

12 It furnishes a habitat and home for delusion;
it brings about distraction of mind
and an end to equanimity.
It is an abode of delirium and sweet madness,
a dangerous enemy of mental concentration.
It is the source of suffering,

the destroyer of happiness,
the domicile of a sinful character.
Marriage, like a demon,
defiles even the sensible
and brings them to ruin.

RATNĀVALĪ (*tearfully, to herself*): I wonder whether he will continue on in this manner.

MAṆICŪḌA: And furthermore, my friend:

13 Even when I am married
I intend to retire to the forest.
What difference does it make
if others fret and grieve about it?

RATNĀVALĪ (*thinking to herself*): It would be good if my dear friend Padmāvatī were to emulate the Prince in this regard!

GAUTAMA: O,

14 Why when faced with the thought of marriage
are you plagued by such fear,
praising a forest hermitage in words so exalted,
foregoing the veneration of your feet
by the beams pouring forth from the jewels
on the heads of the vassal kings,
and relinquishing the joys of royal sovereignty?

MAṆICŪḌA: Is there then any place more worthy of praise than the forest? Listen here!

15 Could that same joy then rule supreme
in the precincts and quarters
of the heavenly Nandana grove,
where the slates and rock slabs are as soft
as the buttocks of the female deities —
joy such as is felt in woodlands,
lonely, lovely, and blessed
where droves of gazelles dwell and romp
in their abundant innocent charm.

And furthermore, my friend:

16 The vast and vaulted mountain caves,
wondrously deep and blessed
by the presence of human beings rich in austerities,
girded by verdant forest borders
and near the banks of rivers,
appear to call out to the wayfarers
in the voices of the waterfalls,
sweet as tambourines:
"We lie beyond all reach
of the fire of the defilements!"

RATNĀVALĪ (*to herself*): Alas, how somber is his talk!

GAUTAMA: O you who are so devoid of compassion — you have not the slightest feeling of sympathy for those of your family!

MAṆICŪḌA: As for sympathy for my earthly relatives, the matter stands as follows:

17 All human beings are heir and subject
to constant flux and change.
They come into being moment after moment
like lamps of oil and soon perish once again
due to a lack of the oil of love.
Only those escape suffering
for whom rebirth is no more.

Furthermore, my friend, the following holds true as long as one does not regard greed as the basis for sympathy:

18 After having been sprinkled
with the water of greed,
from the seed of earlier as yet unused deeds,
covered over by the dust of ignorance,
sprouts forth the shoot of rebirth.

RATNĀVALĪ (*thinking to herself*): Where can one find such tranquility of mind, even among the holy?

GAUTAMA: Every human being should live his life here on earth in accordance with the norms of the world.

MAṆICŪḌA: What then are these worldly norms?

GAUTAMA: The desire for sensual pleasures.

MAṆICŪḌA: Let the pleasures of the senses be! Ah, let them be. Listen here:

19 The pleasures of the senses
are like poison — Both are sweet

but in the first moment of their tasting;
in their aftermath, when digested,
both are terrible and full of torments.
The dense darkness of delusion is common to both,
and both bring a body to trembling
by their inevitable effect.

And

20 Should one take a closer look, however,
at poison and the pleasures of the senses,
then poison proves to be the better thing
when weighed against
the dangerous sensual pleasures.
For poison's bane is perilous
but in a single round of existence,
while sensual pleasures poison a being
in the incarnation to come as well.

GAUTAMA: Now, now! First just take a look at the face of the girl! Afterwards you two can withdraw to the forest together.

MAṆICŪḌA: That won't do. For

21 "This should be done tomorrow, and that today,
that after a short while, and this immediately."
If a human being thinks such thoughts,
then truly I fear that
the wroth and dreadful God of Death,
whose once black club
has been stained deep crimson
by his grisly sidelong glances,
will laugh at him.

RATNĀVALĪ (*weeping, to herself*): Alas, dear friend and companion! Leading the way I will show you the path to the world beyond.

GAUTAMA (*sobbing*): Alas, does he who would abandon his entire retinue not lack any and all feeling of pity ?

MAṆICŪḌA: I would even offer my own body!

GAUTAMA: For what purpose?

MAṆICŪḌA: For the benefit of others.

GAUTAMA: Perhaps you wish to evade your own duties while worrying about those of others?

MAṆICŪḌA: You simple and vile-minded lout!

22 Even the beasts of the field eat
of their own accord
that grass which is easy to find
or drink water which happens to be at hand
when plagued by a strong thirst.
The specific dignity of man, on the other hand,
consists in this: that he is able to care
about the welfare of others.
Yes, this alone is true happiness and true humanity!

RATNĀVALĪ (*sighing with relief*): The opportunity has been found — the knot tied with the rope of life has been loosened.

GAUTAMA: For what reason do you act for the benefit of others?

MAṆICŪḌA: O you who fail to understand one iota about the benefit of others, behold:

23 The sun, drawn by tireless steeds,
crosses the heavens, giving light to man,
and the "Bearer of Treasures," this earth,
constantly bears its burden of human beings
without counting their numbers. In all of this
there is not a scintilla of selfishness.
And it is precisely the nature of great men
that their sole and distinguishing
trait of character is this desire
for the benefit and happiness
of other human beings.

GAUTAMA (*reflecting to himself*): O you who are so unselfish, which would be deemed more valuable: concern for me, a Brāhman, or for another human being?

MAṆICŪḌA: You have remained long untouched by the feeling of compassion.

24 How could even an ego-centered person be happy
when his heart is consumed by grief
because his kin dwell in this world
in the midst of sorrow?
How then could a noble man,
who bears upon his body
the suffering of all humankind,
ever be joyous, even if he lives
free from the burden of oppression?

RATNĀVALĪ (*thinking to herself*): Here is the opportunity for my longing and desire!

GAUTAMA: Is then all of mankind your kith and kin?

MAṆICŪḌA: Friend, let me describe the situation:

25 From time immemorial, the band of family members
consists of her in whose womb one first was caught,
and her upon whose bosom the husband
took his playful and ardent pleasure,
and finally of all those whose absence
causes deep and lasting grief.

RATNĀVALĪ (*to herself*): O, great is his heart beyond all measure!

GAUTAMA: Why do you stay so far from the world of kin and relatives if this is the world you wish to help?

RATNĀVALĪ (*to herself*): Now he has spoken well-chosen words!

MAṆICŪḌA (*sighing deeply*): Most difficult it is to find a human being who requests a clear and specific thing.

GAUTAMA: What is meant by the expression "thing?"

MAṆICŪḌA: The request for something; for example, for a life.

GAUTAMA: And who is the greatest among those humans who are helpful and cooperative?

RATNĀVALĪ (*to herself*): That was an excellent question!

MAṆICŪḌA: He who is a place of refuge for every person plagued by suffering.

RATNĀVALĪ (*to herself, filled with great joy*): Now I finally have the opportunity I've been hoping for!

The Vidyādharī bows blushing with shame and expresses her homage.

RATNĀVALĪ (*weeping*): Since I am gravely grieved, you are my ultimate place of refuge! O mighty one, unfortunate is the fate I have suffered. Have pity on me!

MAṆICŪḌA (*highly pleased, looks at her*): My dear woman, do not be afraid!

26 I am friend of each and every man —
to help humankind is my heartfelt desire.
Do not be afraid,
O dark-eyed daughter, do not fear.
Tell me quickly what is to be done!

GAUTAMA (*to himself, full of astonishment*): Where does this beautiful creature come from, she who beams forth a splendor so magnificent?

MAṆICŪḌA: Tell me, what favor do you desire of me?

RATNĀVALĪ (*lifting her head and gazing upon him full of passion*): Great and mighty one: your body!

The Vidūṣaka finds this intolerable. He is greatly displeased.

GAUTAMA (*to himself*): This indeed is like the behavior of a bewitching Vidyādharī. I will speak about this now. (*Aloud*) O friend, be up and away! This is a viṣakanyā, a maiden of poison. I suspect, my dear friend, she will ask you for your body.

RATNĀVALĪ (*anxiously, to herself*): How has this man recognized me in my altered appearance? After all, I've disguised myself as a distinguished woman, and this in order to attain more perfectly the goal my dear friend seeks.

MAṆICŪḌA (*happily, to himself*): O sister, you who request my body, now I finally behold a supplicant who is also a person endowed with eloquence!

GAUTAMA (*lifting a club into the air*): Away with you! Be gone, you maiden of poison! Do you dare to request the body of my dear friend, a man fit to bear the burden of a royal sovereignty stretching across the planet?

MAṆICŪḌA: How can you curse a supplicant? (*Turning his back to the Vidūṣaka, joyfully*) My good woman, are you truly asking for my body?

RATNĀVALĪ: O great and mighty one, this is not a request that might allow of another boon or remedy. If the mere sight of your body puts an end to the torments suffered by another, then you should allow that person to stay in your presence!

MAṆICŪḌA (*saddened*):

27 To break my word to a person
so cunningly gifted in the art of words
is not my nature.
But how much less in my nature it is
to grant the fulfillment of such a wish!

RATNĀVALĪ (*weeping*):

28 My friend, of whom I've grown so fond,
is suffering from severe pains in the head.
For this there is no other relief or remedy
than to behold your very person.

GAUTAMA (*fearfully*): Alas, first she creates the impression she is speaking on her own behalf, and then changes her tack; it's her friend she means.

MAṆICŪḌA (*without hearing what the Vidūṣaka has said*): Tell me, where then is your friend, of whom you've grown so fond?

RATNĀVALĪ: She lives upon the summit of Mt. Himavant.

MAṆICŪḌA (*calling her up the slope of the pleasure hill*): Let's leave now and go there!

RATNĀVALĪ: Who would think a great and mighty monarch, crossing the firmament with his royal retinue, is something commonplace?

The two pantomime flight by means of dance gestures.

GAUTAMA (*calling out*): You two are now departing, leaving me — a Brāhman — in the lurch: just as if you were brushing aside some useless clump of dirt.

MAṆICŪḌA: My friend, you too should rise into the air!

The Vidyādharī, seeing that the Vidūṣaka is filled with great fear, smiles, takes him by hand and walks with him about the stage.

MAṆICŪḌA (*astonished*): Friend, look and behold!

29 The disk of the sun appears to plunge from the sky
and hurls itself down upon our heads.
The earth with all its mountains sinks from view;
the dark blue tamāla forests are skirted
by rows of clouds scattered and dispersed.

GAUTAMA: No matter how great your wonderment may be — I for one am a Brāhman, and so I too will embark for one mountain or another, setting out upon the path of the mendicant and taking with me a vessel of water!

MAṆICŪḌA: Don't be afraid — now behold something quite astonishing:

30 We see quite clearly
a mountain resembling a high tower
pressed up against a canopy of passing clouds;
we see the river, whose banks are outlined
by a row of ducks, like a highway
upon which the dust swirls upward;
we behold the ocean ringed
by the Cakravāḍa Mountains,
much like a moat with a wall of exceeding height.
We observe the disk of the earth
as like unto a single city.

RATNĀVALĪ: O, the Prince has observed all with great care!

The Vidūṣaka sees the surface of the earth far below him in giddy depths, and looks with an expression of great inner fear at the other figures up on high.

GAUTAMA (*in great anxiety*): O, what is this thing approaching us from out of the firmament like all the white summits of Mt. Himavant, filling the entire sky?

RATNĀVALĪ (*mocking him*): Yes, Brāhman, this is precisely their distinguishing feature.

MAṆICŪḌA (*looking in that direction*): These most certainly are the stars!

GAUTAMA: How is it that the stars have such an expanse?

MAṆICŪḌA: They always have such a gigantic range and spread.

GAUTAMA: Why then do they appear so small from the earth?

MAṆICŪḌA: When seen from afar they appear minute indeed.

GAUTAMA: But how is it possible then that they move across the heavens without tumbling down?

MAṆICŪḌA: Though born aloft in soaring heights, we likewise do not fall.

GAUTAMA: Why is it then that they remain invisible by day?

MAṆICŪḌA: If you come closer to the stars, you can see them in daytime as well.

RATNĀVALĪ: I think the Prince has seen all this before!

GAUTAMA: O dear friend, how comes it that we hear a roaring sound, as if sea waves were being churned by a mighty wind?

MAṆICŪḌA (*reflecting*): This is the sound of the heavenly Ganges. For

31 From out of the multitude of all the beings
we behold in the heavens,
it is the elephants of the celestial region
that playfully squirt in their frolic
water from their trunks,
drinking their fill of the droplets.
They have left the divine river of the Ganges,
lying there like Śeṣa, snake of the worlds.
Whereupon the Seven Rishis,
that Great Bear, enter the Ganges
to bathe in its waters, wearing golden lotuses,
and the droplets upon them sparkle
like the rays of pearls.

The Seven Rishis deserve our homage!

After these words, all pay homage to the Seven Rishis.

From inside the dressing room:

32 So that he might bring benefit to all mankind,
Maṇicūḍa shall receive two further crest-jewels:
a jewel of a wife, and a jewel-like son,
and both shall be equal to him in birth and station!

RATNĀVALĪ (*joyfully to herself*): These Seven Rishis, in and through the clarity of their words, have become like the grantors of wish and desire!

GAUTAMA: Our ability to fly has brought us to this place — let us rest a while and tarry on the banks of the heavenly Ganges!

Final Verse

33 May this place —
praised by all the dispassionate Bodhisattvas,
where the melodious songs of the poets resound —
be ever victorious!
For this reason did Candragomin
compose this play,
deriving its moral teaching from the school
of the vehicle of the Self-Born Svayambhū,
the Tathāgata Departed in Perfection.

All exit.

End of Act Two

ACT THREE

Enter Mādhavī.

MĀDHAVĪ (*tearful, to herself*): After Ratnāvalī departed from this place, I was able to calm Padmāvatī's troubled mind to some extent for only one short day. Now, as a result, her head throbs all the more. Ever since Ratnāvalī left, so long ago, my friend and companion Padmāvatī has hardly been able to bear her heavy sorrow. Her eye is blinded by the prospective happiness of the possible pleasure of royalty. She is like one who has plunged headlong into the water — in her tearful and weeping way of life, her heart is filled with profound suffering.

Those who desire the fruition of their personal and private goals are not even aware of what is most important to achieve this. Even should Ratnāvalī return, it will be fruitless and without avail. I will speed to my dear friend as soon as I have found a means to alleviate her sorrow.

As she walks around, looking about, she spies her dear friend Padmāvatī leaning upon Bindumatī, who is sitting upon flagstones fashioned from moonstone gems at the foot of a pārijātaka tree. She steps up to them.

You're all alone here at the edge of the wilderness!

Padmāvatī and Bindumatī appear, looking around the area a bit.

PADMĀVATĪ (*sighing pensively*): He who is noble, the Flower Arrowed One — Kāma, the Lord of Love, most likely did not even feel the smart and sensations when his body was being consumed by the fire. Had he felt it, how could he now burn and torture others?

MĀDHAVĪ (*approaching her*): Dearest friend, is your depression now over and past?

Padmāvatī repeats the words she has just uttered.

BINDUMATĪ: Hey there, Padmāvatī, why don't you pay any attention to her? After all, she's your dear friend!

PADMĀVATĪ (*excited*): Tell me! Where, O where is my dear friend Ratnāvalī?

BINDUMATĪ: No, it's not Ratnāvalī; this is Mādhavī.

PADMĀVATĪ (*ashamed, to herself*): I have committed a terrible and grievous offense against the general rules of propriety! (*Aloud*) Friend Mādhavī, this great sorrow which torments me has left me completely confused and bewildered.

MĀDHAVĪ: My dearest companion, be calm and at ease! I have moistened these lotus leaves for you, and they are now as refreshing as the words of noble-hearted humans.

PADMĀVATĪ: O, take them away! Even upon the cool crystal tiles I feel as if I were on fire. Bring some sandal water!

The two sprinkle her with some sandal water.

MĀDHAVĪ and BINDUMATĪ: Even when we let sandal water drip down into the cleavage between your breasts, the inordinate fire of your grief dries it away in throes of torment.

PADMĀVATĪ (*agonizing*): O take it away! Pour it out upon the crystal tiles!

MĀDHAVĪ and BINDUMATĪ (*sobbing, to themselves*): Alas, her mind has once more gone astray! (*Aloud*) Dear companion, in an unbroken stream of droplets a misty spray sprinkles forth from these crystal tiles!

PADMĀVATĪ: Enough of all this! Now I wish to see the portrait painted by Ratnāvalī!

MĀDHAVĪ and BINDUMATĪ (*look at one another, and think full of joy to themselves*): Could it be that the pain in her head now is gone? (*Aloud*) Dear friend, as far as the portrait is concerned, it is still here!

PADMĀVATĪ: But where then is his portrait?

MĀDHAVĪ and BINDUMATĪ: Do not think that it has disappeared —why, it's right under your nose!

PADMĀVATĪ (*pondering the portrait for a long time, to herself, weeping*): The man whose painted portrait looks like this need but hear the lament of an unloved person, and he will always feel compassion—how clearly this is expressed here! (*Gazing up toward the heavens:*)

1 O most excellent and admirable one,
has Kāma, the One with the Five Arrows,
now lost his arrows because of you?
Or has he who found pleasure in your virtues
now been burned by them and rendered powerless?
Now that his eyes have seen me,
a creature of the weaker sex,
he displays the pride of a hero.

(*She looks about in all directions.*) Is there any other way of viewing it? (*Embracing the portrait*) He will yet destroy my innermost being!

MĀDHAVĪ (*rising and looking up toward the heavens*): How is it possible — she does not even notice the bird winging its way across the immaculate canopy of the firmament. (*Looking once again at the sky, full of astonishment*) My dearest friend, look there, just look! Upon the spotless canopy of the firmament we see a distinctive flicker and flashing like lightning bolts.

PADMĀVATĪ: Well and good, go ahead gawking at the scenery! After all, it's only sorrow that now torments me, that's all.

MĀDHAVĪ: Now it seems hidden beyond that mountain peak!

BINDUMAṬĪ: (*also looking*): I wonder what this is? (*Approaches Padmāvatī, thinking to herself:*) I'll have to tell my dear friend about this immediately!

The Prince and Ratnāvalī appear once again in their mimed flight. The Prince, Ratnāvalī, and the Vidūṣaka come on stage.

GAUTAMA: O friend, just look! Here you see the signs that mark the abode of a sage. The sky is covered over by a wreath of smoke which rises from a burnt offering, a gently spreading cloud. And even the beasts, which are wont to fight one with another, show in their changed behavior a supreme and consummate love. Such is the nature of a sage's abode.

MAṆICŪḌA: My friend, this wondrous panorama presents itself as follows to our eyes:

2 The tigress, full of warm affections,
licks with closed eyes
the young buck of the gazelle;
the peacock, imbued with
the loving feelings of close kin,
spreads his tail-feathers over the snakes
so as to ward off the heat of the sun;
the lioness, full of love,
watches over and protects
the young calves
of an absent or dead elephant mother
as if they were her own cubs.
The ascetics living in deep mountain caves
at whose dwelling places animals behave like this
shall be victorious!

RATNĀVALĪ (*looking about, thinks to herself*): We have now approached quite near to my dear friend—she who is so like the moon in her beauty, upon whose face is spread sandalwood paste fresh and thick, gleaming like the halo of garlanded beams that surrounds the moon.

GAUTAMA (*greatly astonished*): O friend, look over there! That woman has a face like the moon, casting jewel-like rays that seem to suffuse her entire body as they pour down.

MAṆICŪḌA (*glancing over*): Because she far surpasses the beauty of her peers, do you in your folly think her to be wearing jewels?

3 Other women wish their body
to be touched by jewels.

Upon her, however, you can see no gem,
For her body naturally shines with splendor.

GAUTAMA: We have seen a "wishing flower!"

Padmāvatī and Mādhavī glance to one side.

PADMĀVATĪ: Ratnāvalī is so long in returning!

GAUTAMA: O friend, just so does a voice sound that is pleasing to the ear!

MAṆICŪḌA: If you ask what is meant by a voice pleasing to the ear, O:

4 If a man, here upon this mountain, confused
by this girl's sidelong glances,
turns away from her infatuating eyes
and toward her mellifluous words,
it is as when drunken bees,
tarrying upon the earth
and alighting atop flowers,
turn from the flowers' outer body
toward the sweetness of the honey within.

RATNĀVALĪ: Look, Destiny is favorable towards us!

GAUTAMA (*thinks joyfully to himself*): This is the fruition of my desire—she looks just like the portrait I saw painted on a canvas!

RATNĀVALĪ: O great and mighty sovereign, rest a bit while I speak with her!

MAṆICŪḌA: I'll do as you wish.

The Vidyādharī, extremely pleased, goes to her two companions.

MĀDHAVĪ: My dear friend, look there! Here comes Ratnāvalī!

PADMĀVATĪ: Where! Where is she?

When Mādhavī and Padmāvatī see that she has come all alone, Padmāvatī swoons in a faint.

RATNĀVALĪ (*very frightened*): My dear, your deepest desire has come true!

MĀDHAVĪ: Hear friend, and breathe a sigh of relief! (*Looking at the Vidyādharī:*) O woe is me, miserable one that I am! O woe, o woe! What has happened to her? (*She embraces Padmāvatī and looks at her:*) Has your deepest desire escaped your grasp once again, just when its fulfillment seemed so near?

RATNĀVALĪ: Prince, come to my help! My dear friend is being murdered and carried off by that slayer Yama, God of Death!

MAṆICŪḌA (*dismayed*): Woe, she is bereft of her senses!

GAUTAMA: My friend, make haste!

The two approach the three girls.

RATNĀVALĪ (*bowing to the feet of the Prince*): O great and mighty sovereign, have pity on my dear friend!

MAṆICŪḌA (*fearful and embarrassed*): Advise me what to do!

RATNĀVALĪ: How then could I give that person counsel and advice who has penetrated to the outermost limits of knowledge? Unless he might perchance caress my dear friend and companion with the nectar which pours down like a cooling river from the hand of this great and mighty sovereign!

MAṆICŪḌA (*touching Padmāvatī's head with his hand*):

5 I feel now as though I had been shattered
by this moon-faced woman.
Have I been destroyed by boundless joy
or does my sorrow grow
upon seeing your suffering?

When Padmāvatī opens her eyes a bit, the hero continues:

6 This woman with the eyes of a gazelle,
who has with her fingers smeared
sandalwood paste upon her face,
whose almond-shaped eyes are open wide,
has a countenance like the orb of the moon
whose disc is half hidden
by gleaming white clouds
that float slowly by like those in the sky.

The Vidyādharī, seeing her dear friend revive, is extremely pleased.

MĀDHAVĪ: Oh, how mighty the Prince is!

GAUTAMA: Dear friend, your deepest desire has been fulfilled!

RATNĀVALĪ: This mighty monarch has helped soothe and assuage the pain in Padmāvatī's head. Now he should touch her body with his fingertips!

MAṆICŪḌA (*stroking her body, full of joy*): Let there now be an end to sadness!

7 Gradually and quite perceptibly
her body begins to quiver,
like mālatī blossoms that open at nightfall—
tremulous blossoms shaken by the wings of bees
enticed by their intoxicating fragrance,
much as Padmāvatī's tender body
trembles with great vehemence, her mind
oppressed by a heavy burden.

PADMĀVATĪ'S TWO FRIENDS: Dearest companion, breathe a sigh of relief! You have found favor in the eyes of this great and mighty sovereign. Now that he has beheld you, your most heartfelt desire is as certain as your own body's being.

Timidly Padmāvatī looks over toward Maṇicūḍa. Trembling with embarrassment, she arises and attempts to hurry away, wishing to escape and flee from the spot, but is unable to do so.

RATNĀVALĪ: My dear friend, don't be in such a hurry! Show to him who has just arrived and seated himself your respect and homage!

MAṆICŪḌA:

8 O dark-eyed one, O woman gently trembling
in your grief and great fear,
cease and stop this torment of your body.
The leaves of the garland
which has just broken forth into blossom
are unable to bear and support
even the tremulous feet of the bees.

PADMĀVATĪ (*thinks to herself*): Did this man venture here from the forest, or does it only seem so? Did he appear to me in a dream?

MĀDHAVĪ: Dearest friend, it's truly him! After all, you yourself wove a garland of bakula blossoms to pay homage to the image of the Prince painted on a canvas!

Saying this, she lifts it into the air. Padmāvatī casts a sidelong glance at the hero and then garlands the painting.

MAṆICŪḌA (*studying the painting*): It is an extraordinary likeness. Oh, this is for me a great honor indeed!

GAUTAMA: Since you have always revered the gods in great devotion, you are now rewarded with similar homage.

MAṆICŪḌA: I do only what is fitting and proper.

GAUTAMA: Even the gods grant one's wish if you revere them devotedly. But you are not fulfilling even one single wish so fervently desired by this hermit. Her dear companion spoke quite tellingly about this matter.

MAṆICŪḌA (*smiling*): Do you know perhaps how one might satisfy her wish in a manner proper and fitting?

GAUTAMA: I as a Brāhman will fulfill the wish if you but concur with me.

MAṆICŪḌA: Then I shall concur with you.

GAUTAMA: And I then shall present you to the girl as the object of her desire!

MAṆICŪḌA: You're a vile, deluded, crafty fellow!

GAUTAMA: And you are absolutely intolerable!

MAṆICŪḌA: My friend, even one whose intentions are completely pure and honorable would by this gift gain too much. Behold:

9 Under a pretext she shows me her body,
and then bashfully hides it again;
she throws at me a clearly affectionate glance,
and then restrains it immediately;
she will not allow me to look at her,
and then eagerly longs for my glance.
This young girl bears love in her heart,
and yet does not abandon cunning!

From inside the dressing room a loud cry is heard. All rise in trepidation.

GAUTAMA (*looking in that direction*):

10 This is the sound of a
rut-maddened elephant who has come
running headlong from somewhere in the forest.
Fiercely he twists and turns his dangerous trunk;
squirting water he thunders by
like a violent cloudburst,
and the bees fly in pursuit
of the rut-juice running down his face.

Loud shouts are heard from the dressing room.

GAUTAMA (*in great fear*): O friend, save us!

Filled with terror, Padmāvatī embraces the Prince.

MĀDHAVĪ and BINDUMATĪ: Great and mighty monarch, protect our dearest friend!

MAṆICŪḌA: Don't be afraid!

11 By the strength within my breast
I have held back and detained
this dangerous, wild and rut-maddened elephant,
armed with tusks like thunderbolts
that gleam like thunderbolts as well.

RATNĀVALĪ: What has happened to this threat?

From the dressing room:

12 You who grant to men the boon of fearlessness,
and delight to the triple world,
you are to them a friend,

a ship that carries all sentient beings
across the waves and eddies
of the turbulent sea of suffering.
Could there still be any reason
for the world to fear
the tusks of the elephant,
thrashing wildly back and forth,
when your hand, its ornaments glistening,
twists and turns to and fro
in the gesture granting fearlessness?

MAṆICŪḌA: O, my love, let go of me! The raging elephant has disappeared.

RATNĀVALĪ (*smiling*): Does she even now still cling to your body tightly, from tip to toe?

MAṆICŪḌA (*to himself*): What if I am now seen caught up in so embarrassing a situation! This ill comports with my previous manner and conduct.

Enter the disciple of the sage.

DISCIPLE (*filled with consternation*): Woe! For what reason do even the droves of forest animals — seized by tremendous fear — dart and scramble back and forth in derangement and disarray? Is it true that even the younger disciples of the ascetic, frightened by the elephant, have openly shed their tears? And where has Padmāvatī gone? (*Lost in these thoughts, he walks across the stage. Seeing Padmāvatī, he calls out indignantly*) O Brāhman, Brāhman! Someone in wanton sacrilege has broken into a meditation grove!

All are seized by a great fear.

MĀDHAVĪ and BINDUMATĪ: The disciple of the venerable sage!

Padmāvatī lets go of the Prince and stands there, her face turned toward the ground in bashful shame.

VOICE (*from inside the dressing room*): What, O what has this dangerous elephant done to my daughter Padmāvatī?

Thus weeps the sage.

DISCIPLE (*weeping*): Help, master, help, O help! Padmāvatī is being ravished and defiled!

MĀDHAVĪ and BINDUMATĪ (*to themselves, frightened*): This is most unfortunate!

MAṆICŪḌA (*to himself*): I've fallen into a sorry plight! This has all the earmarks of adverse and inauspicious fate.

GAUTAMA (*angered*): Hey there, black and wicked Brāhman, why do you weep and utter falsehoods! (*Saying this, he lifts up his cudgel and approaches him.*)

DISCIPLE (*shouting*): O Brahmā! O woe is me! Master, help!

Enter the sage.

SAGE (*angrily*): Who's that? (*Saying this, he looks about, claps his hands together, and stamps his feet on the ground.*)

13 Have then the gods — one and all — been destroyed?
Have the imprecations lost their power and potency,
so that some mere intruder is able to harrass and
defile the community of ascetics?

Continuing:

Alas, O daughter Padmāvatī! Since I intended Padmāvatī for the Prince Maṇicūḍa, I now feel a deep pang of sorrow!

MAṆICŪḌA:

14 O Being perfect and sublime! Great holy man,
who is so grieved because of me!
Transgressions against the commandments
of good conduct are always distressing to others.
But should my deeds offend good conduct,
then even the gods shall learn of it!

GAUTAMA (*in great anxiety*): Yet what does one do in such a situation?

SAGE: The gods of the sages have full knowledge regarding each and every human!

GAUTAMA: Deceitful Brāhman, disappear and be gone! Is there any god whose power is greater than that of the Master?

SAGE:

15 Should the gods this instant
plummet to the earth?
Should the seething ocean dry up
in the span of a second?
Or should the world-consuming conflagration
turn all humankind to ashes with its flaming rays,
like the burning of grass?

RATNĀVALĪ (*thinks to herself*):

16 By his glance alone
this sage has the power to poison.
Since the venom of his curse
has not been rendered harmless and ineffective,
I must now clear up the apparent offense.

She approaches and pays homage to the sage.

O father, forgive me, forgive me. This great and mighty sovereign has preserved Padmāvatī from being killed by a rut-maddened elephant bolting forth from the hermitage!

SAGE: And who is he?

GAUTAMA (*as if he were afraid*): The son of the sovereign Brahmadatta — Maṇicūḍa.

SAGE: Is it true that this man is Prince Maṇicūḍa? (*He observes him more carefully and weeps.*) An end to all doubts!

17 This youth is of incomparable beauty,
and upon his head he bears a jewel
as his characteristic sign
distinguishing him from all others.
How can I have mistaken
a wishing tree for a tree of poison?

Turning toward all present:

18 I am simple-minded, impatient and ignorant;
in my simplicity I give
in all too easily to my desires;
and due to my complete and total lack
of any formal education,
I have let my transgressions come to light.

Lifting his hands and joining his palms in the añjali gesture:

O my son-in-law, you who are famous among men, may you forgive these my trespasses! They were only committed out of ignorance!

GAUTAMA (*to himself*): The Brāhman is reviving!

MAṆICŪḌA: Among the exalted there are no trespasses!

The Brāhman embraces the Vidūṣaka joyfully.

DISCIPLE and GAUTAMA (*to each other*): You too should forgive!

SAGE: Behold, the Prince has been given to Padmāvatī by the powers of fate!

19 O daughter Padmāvatī, the "master of your life"
has now become your husband and consort.
Put an end to embarrassment and shame,
and rejoice from the depths of your heart!

MAṆICŪḌA (*to himself*): All this has certainly come about rather quickly! (*Aloud*) O noble one, forgive me! I follow the old-fashioned practice of showing respect and homage to parents!

SAGE: Let the cloud of your hand grow full with the water of nuptial benediction, and then go forth from here united with your bride!

MAṆICŪḌA (*pondering*): Oh noble-minded one, I am of the warrior caste!

SAGE: And this child has been born from the cup of a lotus blossom floating upon Lake Mānasa!

GAUTAMA: Just so have we heard!

MAṆICŪḌA: Noble one, I lack the consent of my parents!

GAUTAMA: You have their unconditional consent! As far as their agreement is concerned, they presented Padmāvatī to you as your bride the moment they received her picture!

SAGE: And there is no additional objection?

MAṆICŪḌA: Shame.

SAGE: Why is that?

MAṆICŪḌA: When one behaves as I do!

SAGE: What is the reason for such behavior?

MAṆICŪḌA: Well, precisely this: That I do not wish to marry!

GAUTAMA (*weeping*): O if you do not even wish to protect the life of one who is attached to you, you will destroy her, and with her the entire family of the sage!

RATNĀVALĪ (*weeping*): Now he will leave us all!

SAGE (*weeping*): Will not she whose body is like yours (in beauty) be ruined, even if she lives a moral life? If you act against our wishes, simply because you have seen our immense pleasure, and if you pour excessive insult upon me by this abuse, tormenting me unduly and proving me a fool, then we — together with our entire retinue — shall cast ourselves as a burnt offering into the fire! O, someone go and fetch fire!

DISCIPLE: Since I find this sight unbearable, I will be the first to throw myself into the flames!

GAUTAMA (*thinking to himself*): Your character is admirable!

MAṆICŪḌA (*to himself*): Indeed, everyone here seems to be growing very agitated! (*Aloud*)

20 O noble-minded one,
never will I ever say:
"I have nothing at all to give!"
Since, on the contrary,
I am filled with compassion,
I will sacrifice my very self for her sake.

PADMĀVATĪ (*to herself*): Thus he has made me his bride! My happiness knows no measure!

SAGE: You and Padmāvatī shall live together according to the moral precepts, and shall not surrender yourselves to anything unwholesome.

GAUTAMA: Is it not true that you have not yet even attained liberation for yourself — you who seek to liberate others?

MAṆICŪḌA: Say what you like!

The Vidūṣaka and Brāhman dance about.

RATNĀVALĪ (*to herself*): My Creator is well disposed toward me!

SAGE:

21 Like me, Maṇicūḍa has made
the Lord of the Mountains his bride,
out of a feeling of love
and based on his knowledge
of the moral precepts.
But he has not been mindful
of the mountain —
that is to say the life of a hermit —
to the same extent that I have.

He then enters the house of sacrifice, and meditates according to the prescribed rules, while all the others, having received his blessing, walk about.

SAGE (*looking up to the heavens*): Has the day come to an end? For:

22 When day is done and the vicula forests gleam
blue-black in the dusk,
the elephant herds, with drooping eyes,
drunk with sleep
migrate from the riverbanks
to their places of rest
in the mountain valleys and gorges.
Having gathered and chopped up

the crackling branches of the śalmalī tree—
their burden of firewood—
the ascetics find their senses at peace,
and the intoxicating fragrance
of guggulu flower-dust
wafts in all directions.

Final Verse

23 By means of this play,
composed with crystal clarity
by that moon among noble-hearted men,
Candragomin, and now being presented
on this stage by the players,
one attains a gem of unsurpassed value:
that supreme form of knowledge
which has as its object the dispassionate one,
the model of men, the Victorious Buddha.

After this verse all exit.

End of Act Three

ACT FOUR

Entr'acte

Enter Mādhavī.

MĀDHAVĪ (*weeping, to herself*): My dear friend Padmāvatī has been away now for more than a year, and I, unhappy soul, don't know whether I will ever see her again. I feel so lonely in this meditation grove, though many ascetics dwell here. I should therefore either suppress my sorrow, or go off to a secluded spot and there cry out my heart. I must decide what to do! (*Immersed in these thoughts, she walks about the stage.*) Here is the santāna tree that was planted in this park when my dear friend was still a child. And look, why here is the mādhavī climbing ivy! Unfortunate soul that I am, I planted it together with Padmāvatī right next to the tree. (*Saying this, she embraces the climber and weeps.*) Where has my dearest friend gone? O you trees, is it fitting that your buds should blossom now? Or has Padmāvatī also experienced a birth? (*Her thoughts continue:*) The other trees glisten with a similar brightness, as though they had heard some such tidings.

VOICE (*from within the dressing room offstage*): A miracle! A great man has been born!

Upon hearing this, Mādhavī looks around and observes the Brāhman Mauñja entering onstage.

MAUÑJA: O, a great man has been born!

Mādhavī approaches the venerable Mauñja and pays him homage.

MAUÑJA (*joyfully*): Congratulations! Your dear friend Padmāvatī has given birth to a son!

MĀDHAVĪ (*in great joy*): Mauñja, you cause a stream of nectar to rain down upon me! And what name, with great ceremony, was given to the child?

MAUÑJA: Padmottara.

MĀDHAVĪ: O joy, O joy!

MAUÑJA: And do you think this is the only bit of joyous news?

MĀDHAVĪ: But this is more than enough! What other glad tidings have you to report?

MAUÑJA: After beholding the face of the boy, King Brahmadatta, filled with great joy, sanctified the Prince Maṇicūḍa as sovereign.

MĀDHAVĪ: O joy, O joy!

MAUÑJA: Then Kāntimatī and King Brahmadatta went off to the forest of the ascetics. And soon after, Prince Maṇicūḍa, following his father, also went there.

MĀDHAVĪ (*tearful*): Mauñja, did my dear friend perhaps do this as well?

MAUÑJA: Listen first to how this story ends! King Brahmadatta then ordered an ascetic's grove to be installed in the park of his palace garden in order to banish the world-weariness of the Prince, and the King now lives in this grove. Prince

Maṇicūḍa is just about to perform an unlimited and supreme sacrifice, the sacrifice known as the *nirargaḍa* sacrifice, carrying out the command of your father, and I too will hasten there. What news should I bring to your dear friend?

MĀDHAVĪ: The following: Become as before the ornament in the ascetic's abode!

MAUÑJA: This base woman is a destroyer of Padmāvatī's happiness!

MĀDHAVĪ (*to herself, extremely frightened*): What have I said? (*Aloud*) Let us enter this grove! You must give her another message!

Exit Mādhavī and Mauñja.

End of Entr'acte

Enter servant.

SERVANT: Be off with you, get out of here! O why do people give them anything when all they want is more and more? Do people do anything in that house of Brāhmans, for all their bustling and running about? (*Looking around*) How can all these Brāhmans — so difficult to satiate and satisfy, wanting to eat each and every thing — run all about, never staying in one place? First they grasp one thing in their hands, then put it aside for another, then take hold of a third, and this though everything here must be watched and guarded. And how can it be that while some make sacrifices, others sit down upon the lion's throne, though they are nothing more than vagabonding Brāhmans? Go away, be gone, get out of here, you pack of Brāhmans! Get going and be on your way! (*He acts as though he were suffering from the wounds of a malediction.*) You rogues and rascals, are you perhaps threatening me? (*Seeing Maṇicūḍa's Prime Minister Subāhu approaching, he thinks:*) They will certainly complain to him about me!

Enter Subāhu.

SUBĀHU: Hey there, you ugly fellow, be on your way, off with you and be gone! Why do you insult the beggars here? We are happy to give them whatever they wish for. The following should be undertaken for their benefit and advantage: King Maṇicūḍa will take direct responsibility for all the *nirargaḍa* sacrifices from this moment on, and it is therefore of great importance to him that by dint of his sovereignity he should with these gifts fulfill the wishes of all men. For that reason, the supplicants should be given even the smallest thing they desire in this sacrificial ceremony. In accordance with the rules that were established previously, they will receive what they desire. This practice, intended for their benefit, has not arisen suddenly, as something out of the ordinary; rather, it has continued down into the present after having been initiated by King Maṇicūḍa five years ago.

SERVANT (*to himself*): No matter how furious this man is, the supplicants here will receive nothing at all!

He runs from the scene.

SUBĀHU (*walking about the stage, to himself*): Since I have been charged by King Maṇicūḍa with the task of looking after gifts, I'll take a closer look at them now. (*Gazing about, very pleased*) The enormous riches of the sovereign have not been depleted by the fact that each and everyone, as planned, has taken what he desired. For:

1 The heaps of gold here are exceedingly high,
rivaling Mt. Meru in their loftiness,
and the radiant mound of precious stones
shames even the splendor of the sun.
The glittering piles of necklaces,
heaped layer upon layer,
form with their choice round pearls
a garland of stars.
People gather from this store without limitation,
and stroll about in ease and comfort,
as though they were in their own homes.

He walks around, observes something else, and then thinks to himself:

2 Because they smell the odor of
the intoxicating rut-juice of the best elephants,
trickling to the ground in an unceasing flow,
the long-limbed horses
trip upon their hooves and stumble.
We hear the tinkle of small bells
set to ringing by the motion
of the wondrous wagons
decked out with splendid silk banners.

The great earth, bearing all its treasures,
appears to tremble from the din of the wheel rims,
set to turning by the Brāhmans.

Since he has presented the hecatomb of a hundred offerings of Śatakratu, I must call him a god tarrying here upon the earth! (*He looks at something else and thinks to himself:*) I wonder whether such a distinguishing mark as his crest-jewel would not be insufferable for a certain Kuru king named Duṣprasaha, whose name itself signifies "insufferable". I'm sure he won't be able to stand it at all! (*Walking about:*) Over there the King himself has entered the house of alms.

3 In the distinctive radiance
of his beauty and in his love,
he surpasses even the tranquility of Brahmā.
With his truthfulness
he has conquered all the world,
and lives now as the moral law made flesh.

He sets out toward the house of alms. King Maṇicūḍa, Padmāvatī, the Vidūṣaka and the sacrificial priest now appear. After Subāhu has drawn near to the King and the sacrificial priest who stands near the place of offerings, he pays them homage.

May His Majesty be victorious, may he be victorious! Having been dispatched with the royal order, I have inspected the sites for the alms.

MAṆICŪḌA:

4 Is it true that the supplicants enter there
as if the house were their very own;
that they receive whatsoever they desire,
thus fulfilling their most heartfelt wishes?

SUBĀHU: The fulfillment of their desire is perfect and complete.

5 The wealth which the kings have garnered
with great effort and travail
from all quarters of the globe
has been placed at the comfortable disposal
of one and all.
Since the people entered into every (store)house
and helped themselves most generously,
they now possess
much more than even you.

MAṆICŪḌA: That's not true at all! The material objects here belong to one and all alike. In what sense did I make a gift? These things are also at the disposal of all other human beings. And even those objects that I myself control and determine have become in equal measure the means of my generosity—this is what I have had proclaimed. Behold:

6 These material objects,
held in high esteem throughout the world,
have led human beings astray
by awakening their greed.
Thus it is that men now believe
in the existence of an ego.

On the other hand, I

7 would willingly and at all times
surrender even this my body,
devoid of value and remembrance,
in order to attain some benefit
for sentient beings. Whosoever
desires this body, no matter in
what way, shall enjoy the right
to use it in the manner desired!

Confused shouting is heard from the dressing room. Seized by great anxiety, all look up toward the heavens. The eye of the King twitches ominously, and the people tremble.

PRIEST (*carrying out the sacrifice in deferential zeal*): Ā śrauṣaṭ ā śrauṣaṭ.

GAUTAMA: How astonishing, how very astonishing!

8 The earth, together with all its human beings,
shakes and quakes beyond all measure,
like a ship passing through
the tempestuous waters of the ocean,
churned by the fierce winds
and swirled by a wreath of waves.

MAṆICŪḌA: Friend, you have observed well:

9 The whole earth heaves like the storm-tossed waves
of a sea churned by violent winds.
This is why it resembles a ship now tossed on high,

now plummeting into the depths.
The people reel and stagger about
as though intoxicated by wine.

PADMĀVATĪ: O where has our son Padmottara run off to?

A servant enters, holding Padmottara by the hand.

SERVANT: Padmottara is here!

PADMOTTARA: Honorable father, what does this mean?

PADMĀVATĪ (*grasping the hand of the boy and approaching the king*): My husband, what is the portent of such an earthquake?

MAṆICŪḌA (*grasping Padmāvatī's hand in order to calm her*): O timid one, behold! A miracle unparalleled, which in itself is almost reason to rejoice! For:

10 The course taken by the waves of the tremor,
great and manifold in its depth and height,
resembles a line of moving parasols,
banners, flags, and diadems upon the verandas;
the clap of a loud noise, which rumbles
as violently as thunder from the clouds —
all this seems like an ocean,
and is in reality but the steady and undeviating,
ever manifold planet: the earth.

And furthermore, dear Queen:

11 Rows of houses tumble down,
and then right themselves once more;
the rivers flow upward, taking no other course;
the earth in its upheaval,
bringing forth elevations and depressions
of the most diverse shape and form,
resembles the impression made
by a trembling reflection in a mirror.

SUBĀHU: Sovereign, I too have seen it!

12 The eastern regions and their mountain slopes
sink from sight, while the western zones
climb to the heavens;
seized by the tremors of the quake,
the southern regions sink and disappear,
while the northern lands rise
up to the loftiest heights;
the ocean sags down
at its center, while its edges
are lifted high into the sky.
In all this what is on high
touches and is touched by what lies below,
to the furthest reaches of the ocean
and the quarters of the globe.

MAṆICŪḌA (*greatly astounded*): Go outside and calm the people!

Subāhu exits to carry out the King's command.

MAṆICŪḌA (*offering a sacrifice to the Goddess of the Earth*):

13 Whatsoever there may be of signs ominous
for human beings, may its fruit—
as a demonstration of mercy
befitting my sacrificial offering—
ripen for me alone, and not fall
to the lot of other men!
May all men—though they
may have done wrong—
share here in my advantage,
so that human desire might attain
its full and consummate fruition.

The sacrificial priest carries out the sacrifice full of reverence.

PRIEST (*reciting the Vedic sacrificial formula*): Indrāgaccha / hariva āgaccha / medhātither meṣa / vṛṣaṇaśvasya mene (*He peers into the opening of the hearth and jumps back startled.*)

GAUTAMA (*in great anxiety*): O friend, just look! Ah, look!

14 The sacrificial hearth has burst asunder
and from its midst a creature has come forth!
From its mouth gigantic terrifying teeth protrude;
its crimson eyes resemble
the glowing orb of the sun,
and it emits a great and frightful roaring howl.

A Rākṣasa appears.

RĀKṢASA (*dancing about*): Aho hutam aho dattaṁ huṁ—O, the sacrifice has been made; O, it has been granted!

15 Having appeared, I will destroy them
with my powerful steps.
Rays flashing through the ether will I send!
With my outstretched hand
I shall pull the horizon toward me,
and let all creatures tremble!

MAṆICŪḌA: The saying seems true: "Many devils gather round a person who practices virtue!"

In great fear, Padmāvatī shields the face of the child with her cloak, and hides behind the back of the King.

MAṆICŪḌA: O great being, with what intention have you come?

RĀKṢASA: Having erected a great hall of alms, open and accessible to all, can you still ask what my purpose is?

MAṆICŪḌA (*showing utmost pleasure*): Have you come here to ask for something? Tell me what you desire!

RĀKṢASA: Food!

GAUTAMA (*hiding frightened behind the hero's back*): If it's food you want, go on into the hall of alms!

RĀKṢASA: My food is of another sort.

MAṆICŪḌA: Speak!

RĀKṢASA:

16 Flesh which glistens, freshly cut in pieces
by the blade of a sword, in a goodly amount,
warm and red in color—
that is the food of the Rākṣasas!
O ruler of men! Of what benefit to me
are the various types of human sustenance?

MAṆICŪḌA (*extremely pleased*):

17 Come over here, you clever creature—
your heartfelt wish shall be fulfilled!
Come here! This body is food such as you desire.
I have kept and preserved it
for the benefit of others.
By cutting off some of its flesh,
I will long enjoy the fruits of karmic merit.

PADMĀVATĪ (*weeping*): My husband, what is the meaning of your actions?

MAṆICŪḌA: My queen, this sacrifice will bear rich fruit!

GAUTAMA: O friend, do you want to abandon all other men for the sake of a single creature?

MAṆICŪḌA:

18 In this way I will reject
no living being anywhere.
Only for this reason will I sacrifice myself:
So that this creature's torments
might come to an end and cease.

PRIEST:

19 I will not carry out
such a sacrificial ceremony.
Most certainly this demon has appeared
to take as an offering the cattle
now being slaughtered.
The relevant Vedic prescriptions teach
that he should be given the slaughtered beast.

MAṆICŪḌA:

20 If the creature who desires something
so definite from me
happens to be a demon,
why then I'm also quite pleased
to be dealing with a demon.
Carry out the ceremony with haste,
so that his heartfelt wish
might be soon fulfilled!

Continuing:

21 O Brāhman, why, O why are animals
the only creatures suitable for a Rākṣasa
in a sacrifice? Is some substance
dry and juiceless of any use whatsoever
when you cannot obtain the nectar you deserve?

RĀKṢASA: Hey! How come you're wasting my time with your useless chatter?

MAṆICŪḌA: Fine, then: Devour my body as you desire, at the earliest opportune moment!

PADMĀVATĪ (*weeping*): Then first devour my own body, O wretch that I am!

MAṆICŪḌA: But he asked for mine!

PADMĀVATĪ: True, but this body is also of royal blood, is it not?

RĀKṢASA: Oh, come now, what good is this tendency to fear suffering? It's useless, even harmful. Look here:

22 The flesh of one in grief
leaves a bitter, burning, and astringent taste;
that of a passionate person
is easily digestible and almost juicy;
that of someone timid is dry and desiccated;
that of an angry man is sour,
terribly pungent, tart and not tasty—
after eating it you feel heartburn.
The body of someone with a pleasing nature,
on the other hand, is sweet and gives
the greatest satisfaction to all the senses.

MAṆICŪḌA (*showing great pleasure*): Now after all these years I've finally seen a knowledgeable supplicant! (*With these words he takes a knife and cuts off some of his own flesh.*)

PADMĀVATĪ (*seizing his hand*): My husband, don't act rashly! (*To the Rākṣasa:*) O great and powerful being, spare my husband and take me instead!

PADMOTTARA: Hey, you monster! Spare my father and take me instead!

GAUTAMA: O great being, spare my dear friend and devour me!

MAṆICŪḌA: An end to all this foolish chatter! My Queen, do not stand in the way of the fulfillment of my moral law!

Padmāvatī pantomimes fainting in a swoon. The Vidūṣaka hides the face of the boy in his garment.

MAṆICŪḌA: O great being, make good use of this opportunity and enjoy my flesh!

RĀKṢASA (*to himself*): In this way you are the great being, not I! (*The Rākṣasa acts out in pantomime the devouring of Maṇicūḍa's flesh. Aloud:*) Ah, now I've had my fill for a long, long time to come!

GAUTAMA: Noble protectors of the world, your help, your help! My dear friend is throwing away his life!

PRIEST: What use is it for me to stay on here? (*Exits*)

RĀKṢASA: Now I'm really full and satisfied!

MAṆICŪḌA (*offering him his body, and fainting—in pantomime—in a swoon*): O friend who fosters my salvation, eat to your heart's content!

RĀKṢASA (*thinks to himself*): How great and noble is his conduct! It is not proper that a man of such noble character should unnecessarily grieve and suffer for so long! (*Exits.*) (*After only a moment offstage and invisible to the public, he reappears in the guise of Indra.*) O great King, rise up, rise up!

MAṆICŪḌA: Show me your favor and savor joyfully of my body, as your heart desires!

INDRA: I am no Rākṣasa! I am Indra!

MAṆICŪḌA: Who is this welcome guest?

GAUTAMA: Breathe a sigh of relief! O my dear friend, this being is indeed the King of the Gods, here in person before our very eyes! Sovereign, rise up! O, the conduct of the monarch is lauded as more than divine even in the ranks of the gods!

PADMĀVATĪ (*observing the King, weeping, to herself*): O to think I have seen my husband in this condition, and my body is still whole and uninjured!

MAṆICŪḌA: O ruler among the gods, what brings you here?

INDRA: The earth and Mountain of the Gods, Mt. Meru, quaked before the unshakable strength of your character. And that is why I have come, O King: to reveal to all men your character! Your behavior has delighted my eyes.

GAUTAMA: O my friend, look and behold! Another great miracle: the cluster of clouds is beginning to recede, sending forth a sound, as if set in motion by a strong wind.

MAṆICŪḌA: Alas, are humans being tortured by yet another new affliction?

PADMĀVATĪ: Will someone else now appear here?

GAUTAMA: Look and behold! We see somebody emerging with dazzling, bright gem-like rays, white like the circular crest of the snake-king Vāsuki—glowing white as the full harvest moon; glistening as though adorned with a necklace of stars.

MAṆICŪḌA (*gazing in that direction in great astonishment*): Someone else is making an appearance here!

GAUTAMA: From the surface of the earth there has arisen a woman whose form is like that of the jewel among women, Queen Padmāvatī. O my dear friend, just look!

MAṆICŪḌA (*greatly amazed*):

23 Has Lakṣmī herself arisen here
from the surface of the earth?
Or is this resplendent one the Goddess of Earth,
girded by the ocean?

The Goddess of the Earth now appears and presents Maṇicūḍa with a gift.

GODDESS OF THE EARTH: Come here, noble man! Accept this gift!

MAṆICŪḌA: Ah, you are newly come to this place! I wish to pay you homage, together with that noble "Destroyer of Cities," Indra!

INDRA:

24 Although the Goddess of Earth,
completely pure, has satisfied him
by her offering (of a gift),
as if he were a great being,
he nevertheless feels no
undue happiness or joy.

MAṆICŪḌA: Tell me, why are you trembling once again?

GODDESS OF THE EARTH:

25 Because I recognized
your great and noble character,
I was exceedingly pleased—
hence did the ocean, the mountains,
and the forests shudder and shake.
And I trembled too at the sight
of your wondrous and astonishing sacrificial zeal.
My body is overcome by the weight of great joy.

Now I wish to restore your body by the juice of this nectar!

She rubs the nectar over the hero's body.

GAUTAMA (*joyfully*): My dear friend, you look once more as you did before!

PADMĀVATĪ: Such is the moral strength of my noble consort!

INDRA: With self-castigation as rigorous as this it is the very essence of karma that in a later existence there is no karma whatsoever!

GODDESS OF THE EARTH: Sovereign of the gods! He takes no delight in this at all. Just look:

26 Kauśika, many thousands of times before
has this man brought his body
to fruition in previous births!
And even in those existences

he surrendered his body
as easily as one sweeps away some dirt—
in no way influenced by the ego.

(*Continuing:*) I am deeply impressed by the sight of the King. Now I shall take leave and depart! (*Exits*)

INDRA: You shall enter into heaven by the merit you have accumulated here!

MAṆICŪḌA: Are there supplicants there as well?

INDRA : No.

MAṆICŪḌA: If that is so, I will not go there.

INDRA: Would you be pleased if your parents were to go there?

MAṆICŪḌA: As my parents wish!

INDRA: Then I'll go to them to find out! (*Exits*)

The honorable and childless sage Marīci now enters.

SAGE: O sublime and exalted is the character of the great King! (*Approaching*) O great King, hail unto you!

MAṆICŪḌA (*paying obeisance*): Exalted One, what purpose brings you here?

SAGE: I have come for your wife and son.

PADMĀVATĪ (*to herself*): What is the meaning of this?

MAṆICŪḌA (*joyfully*): O Exalted One, it is given to each and every man to request of me my body or some other boon.

Loud cries are heard from the dressing room.

VOICE: It is not part of the sacrificial ceremony to give away one's wife!

MAṆICŪḌA:

27a And it is not part of the practice
of the moral law
to say when a request is made:
"This will not be given!"

GAUTAMA: Disappear from here and be gone, cursed Brāhman, be gone! Of what use to you is the wife of the King? Request something else!

MAṆICŪḌA: One must not speak in this tone of voice!

27b Great sage, take even that
which is dearest to me,
if you so wish, O Exalted One!

SAGE: My daughter Padmāvatī, my son Padmottara, come over here! The King has given both of you to me!

PADMĀVATĪ (*weeping*): Great King, you are most assuredly master and lord; but ponder well that this means cutting asunder the succession of the royal lineage!

MAṆICŪḌA: I have proclaimed it out of the question for me to refuse a request!

PADMĀVATĪ: Stand up! What use is it for me to weep so and sob? Come over here, my son Padmottara! Since my husband has irrevocably cast us aside, take one last look at your father! You will never see him again!

PADMOTTARA: Why will I never see my father again?

PADMĀVATĪ: Because, dearest Padmottara, we will journey to another place. For your father has disowned and abandoned us.

PADMOTTARA: What will you do, mother?

PADMĀVATĪ: Since he has rejected both of us, I will go too.

PADMOTTARA: And will father come along?

PADMĀVATĪ (*recognizing that Padmottara doesn't understand what's happening*): My son, pay your father your respects!

PADMOTTARA (*placing palms together*): Father, why is mother crying so?

GAUTAMA:

28 Alas, you are devoid of all compassion,
to reject a child while it sobs
and wails so bitterly.
O Padmāvatī, O Padmottara,
you two are innocent and pure!

O Brāhman, let us follow you as well! (*He faints in a swoon, in pantomime.*)

SAGE: Come, my daughter! We have a long journey ahead of us!

MAṆICŪḌA (*touching the crown of Padmottara's head, weeping*):

29 May the gods watch over and protect you,
in the forest or city,
upon the mountain or at sea,
and even while you rest and sleep!
My Queen, wheresoever you sojourn,
may no man lay a hand upon the boy!

PADMĀVATĪ (*sadly*): Are you so sure?

MAṆICŪḌA:

30 You must not trespass against the commandment
of the great sage,
even if it should cost you your life!
Through the merit gained
by satisfying a prominent sage,
whose countenance is bright as fire,
the wishes of all mankind are fulfilled.

SAGE: Daughter, get up! We must be on our way!

MAṆICŪḌA: My Queen, you must go!

PADMĀVATĪ (*paying her respects*):

31 May I then also behave
in this exemplary manner,
which marks a pinnacle
in the history of the warrior caste!

PADMOTTARA: Father once promised he'd make me a gift of a horse — will you give it to me now, since you haven't made the present yet?

MAṆICŪḌA (*embracing Padmottara, weeping*): My son, this sage will give it to you!

PADMOTTARA: Take good care of my horses and elephants, my elephant canopies and saddles, father!

MAṆICŪḌA (*to himself*):

32 When I ponder the pain I feel now,
even a threat to my very life would not be as bad
as is this departure of Padmottara,
the delight of his father.

SAGE: My daughter, come! We must be on our way! (*Padmāvatī grasps the hand of the boy, gazes at the King, and leaves with Marīci.*)

MAṆICŪḌA:

33 Since I am bound to them
by the cord of love,
the sorrow I now feel is great!

Friend, come to your senses!

GAUTAMA (*rising, confused*): You haven't really sent them away, have you?

MAṆICŪḌA (*still filled with grief, ponders*): I must see now what my parents are doing!

Palace retinue appears.

RETINUE: A great miracle, a great miracle! Behold the parents of the King flying up into the heavens!

34 They rest upon the summit of Mt. Meru,
where they have landed in a vehicle
that looks like an aerial chariot,
decorated with a garland of victory banners
set astir by the wings of the geese
who pull the chariot.
Praised by hundreds of joyous celestial saints,
they have now reached the home of the gods.

The King looks on filled with joy. He expresses his homage and repeats the verse.

MAṆICŪḌA (*looking upward, in tears*):

35 Father has departed into the realm of the gods,
and mother has followed him.
Padmottara and the Queen have left the city
and have journeyed
to the dwelling of the Brāhman.
Now my mind is impatient for me too

to take my leave
and make my home on a desolate mountain
set in the midst of a lonely forest.

After saying this, he walks about the stage.

GAUTAMA: O friend, if you are departing too, will you be leaving me — a Brāhman — as well?

MAṆICŪḌA: Just as you wish!

GAUTAMA: Though I am a Brāhman, I will follow you, provided you don't give me to another master as a servant.

MAṆICŪḌA: But you are indeed a Brāhman, and you alone have power to decide to give yourself to another!

PALACE RETINUE: O Prince Maṇicūḍa, are you leaving us too?

36 Is it you then whom the gods
of the forest and of the mountains
shall behold in the future,
as you sit in the mountain caves of this earth,
your eyes closed in meditation?

Final Verse

37 May Candragomin, who abridged
the legend of a Bodhisattva,
and took great pains

to compose from this a drama,
be born again in forms of existence
in which he has become
like the dispassionate ones.
Or may he, tarrying long upon this earth,
continue to proclaim the truths of the Buddha!

Exit all.

End of Act Four

ACT FIVE

Entr'acte

Enter a Vidyādhara.

VIDYĀDHARA (*flying playfully and in good spirits through the sky*): O, the unending fame of King Maṇicūḍa has spread to all the ten directions, filling them totally. For:

1 The great white fame of Maṇicūḍa has embellished
all the quarters of the compass
with its magnificence —
as though adorning them
with white earrings and a white garment.
Thus they display tranquility and smile as well
in all their whiteness.
They are as if saturated with milk-white nectar,
like a great profusion of sandalwood,
and the gleaming white beams of the moon
seem to permeate them.
They tremble as though adorned
with an ample array
of pendent and resplendent white necklaces.

See, O see! As concerns his great and growing fame,

2 The Kinnarīs sing his praises in all directions,
and upon the mountaintops the perfect sages and Vidyādharas proclaim his glory.
Below the earth it is the Nāga kings
who wish to hear of him—
with the flaming rays of their crest jewels,
and their circular snake hoods
relaxed in a gesture of peace.

VIDYĀDHARĪ (*entering*): Though Padmāvatī is not yet a widow, she has left all her royal retinue and at the command of her consort has followed after the great sage together with her small son. What, I wonder, has become of her?

VIDYĀDHARA: While staying in the abode of the honorable Marīci,

3 She is now living once again in a mountain gorge
not far from the Himavant,
and now too once again
a great sage has become her father,
just as in times past she grew close and dear
to her first foster father, Bhavabhūti.
Most certainly the great sage Marīci
only undertook to ask Maṇicūḍa for her
so that she would not fall into another's hands
as a result of Maṇicūḍa's munificence!

VIDYĀDHARĪ (*highly pleased*): Padmāvatī has once again joined her former caste—now the burden of her suffering is not difficult to bear. And did you also learn how King Maṇicūḍa is faring these days?

VIDYĀDHARA:

4 Unaware of where Padmāvatī has been taken
and where she now resides,
Maṇicūḍa has also withdrawn to a mountain cave
not far from her and has there become a hermit.
The exceedingly repugnant King Duṣprasaha,
after seeing the city of Sāketa
which Maṇicūḍa abandoned,
a city rich in sacrificial offerings,
surrounded it with his army.

VIDYĀDHARĪ: O my husband, is it possible to collect his pleasing discourses?

VIDYĀDHARA: They are beyond comprehension, for these are the discourses of the King.

VIDYĀDHARĪ: O my husband, where he has gone . . .

VIDYĀDHARA (*laughing*): . . . is something *you* should be able to tell me!

5 After having beheld the whole of the earth
like some painting viewed
from the vault of heaven
will he now journey
to a peak of the Malaya Mountains,
given a fresh appearance
by the splashing ocean waves,
or to one of the pleasant and wondrous
broad mountain terraces of Mt. Meru?
Will he journey to Mt. Pārijāta,

or to a peak of the Himavant
where the gracious and gleaming hosts
of the perfect dwell in happiness supreme?

VIDYĀDHARĪ: I know a splendid spot to which Maṇicūḍa may have gone the first moment he laid eyes on it.

VIDYĀDHARA:

6 There is an apt saying that
one becomes happy at the mere sight
of virtuous men!

Walking about:

7 Within this mountain grotto,
in which spray from the river Mandākinī,
tossed by the gentle winds, grants cool relief,
and where even the branches of young trees
are heavy with buds, human beings
dwell together in peace with lions.

VIDYĀDHARĪ: This is indeed a venerable spot!

Both show their homage.

VIDYĀDHARA (*looking at the hero*):

8 Here in the cool shade of a devadāru tree,
upon tiles fashioned of jewels and pearls
the youthful Maṇicūḍa sits with legs folded under,
a living incarnation of Brahmā
sitting in a similar position on a lotus.

VIDYĀDHARĪ: His comportment is exceedingly steady, deep and earnest, and he has imbued all the glaciers with his beauty. But from where do the flowers bedecking this noble one come?

VIDYĀDHARA (*looking upward*): How very wondrous!

9 The gods let flowers rain down from the heavens
to honor this man of so noble a character.
Let us now go pick flowers so that
we too might in this way
venerate his person!

The two exit from the stage.

End of the Entr'acte

The hero is seen in a state of meditation.

MAṆICŪḌA (*opening his eyes just slightly*): O these are the four stages of meditation free of materiality:

10 The first is still encumbered
by concepts and considerations,
and is replete with the waves of thought;
the second is full of joy and happiness
and once again replete with waves of thought;
the third is characterized by the destruction
of the desire for happiness,
and the fourth has as its sole and most
sublime characteristic
total tranquility of mind.

GAUTAMA: O friend, after you have attained in this manner the happiness of the first, second, third, and fourth stages of meditation, and have filled and for a time disciplined yourself with this alone, why do you now watch over your new possessions like a merchant, not passing on to me, a Brāhman, even a small morsel of this meditation?

MAṆICŪḌA (*smiling*): My friend, meditation follows upon concentration, and this is why you cannot simply pass it on to another person.

11 When a person endowed with a garland of virtues
enters into the state of meditation,
then every wish that has as its aim
the salvation of all human beings is fulfilled.

GAUTAMA: How does one attain the happiness of meditation?

MAṆICŪḌA:

12 When a person supported
by the teachings of non-duality
has rendered harmless
the weapons of the God of Love
and has thus become his own lord and master,
this happiness wells up from within the spirit,
just as the cool waters of a lake grow clear
when all motion within it has subsided.

GAUTAMA: Does it—for an outsider—differ from the happiness of sensual pleasure?

MAṆICŪḌA: Perhaps you wish to mix nectar and poison?

13 The happiness of meditation
cools and refreshes the spirit;
the pleasures of the senses, on the other hand,
render the spirit feeble and faint,
and encircle it with the fires
of sexual desire and hate,
which burn in the spirit like hellfire.

GAUTAMA: If this be so, then I too wish to meditate!

MAṆICŪḌA: Do it then!

Attempting to meditate, the Vidūṣaka hears a noise.

GAUTAMA: O, I hear a sound something like sobbing!

MAṆICŪḌA: Ah yes, meditation is indeed a most wonderful thing!

GAUTAMA: Speak: Didn't you hear anything at all?

MAṆICŪḌA (*hearing something*): That is not just any sound. I'm sure as well that that is a woman weeping!

GAUTAMA: How can you tell?

MAṆICŪḌA:

14 Women have a sonorous voice—
seductive, penetrating, soft and tender—
while that of men is agitated, strident, shrill
and rough beyond all measure.

My friend, this sounds like a soft voice quite near.

GAUTAMA: I believe the sound of this voice resembles one I've heard in the past.

MAṆICŪḌA: I have the same impression. Most likely it is some female ascetic tormented by suffering whom we hear weeping. It is only proper that we should hurry to her side.

GAUTAMA: Friend, what good can it possibly do to look into the matter?

From within the dressing-room:

O exalted protectors of the world, help, O help!

MAṆICŪḌA: When a person finds herself in such dire straits, it is only fitting and proper that we pay a modest bit of heed!

GAUTAMA: Then are you like an impudent novice, constantly and evermore wanting to cause yourself grief and worry due to the suffering of others?

MAṆICŪḌA: Friend,

15 For countless ages the self has in this way
come into being again and again
within the round of existence.
He who is not a friend of every sentient being
has nowhere a friend.

The two rise in great agitation and walk back and forth.

GAUTAMA: O! Is this not a likeness of Queen Padmāvatī?

MAṆICŪḌA: What is that you say? Could the place where Queen Padmāvatī is dwelling be the very same in which we also find ourselves?

Padmāvatī appears, followed by two wild forest dwellers of the Śabara tribe.

ŚABARAS: Get going, move along! (*In a loud voice*) You mean you don't want to go?

FIRST ŚABARA: This woman who has been captured shall become the wetnurse for my young son!

SECOND ŚABARA: We've both caught this little calf, and first we have to get her to walk. Get going there!

PADMĀVATĪ (*weeping*): O my husband, you have such a benevolent nature! Do you not wish to save me, an unfortunate woman caught in so distressing a situation?

GAUTAMA: O why should there be any further doubt? It is indeed the Queen, Padmāvatī!

MAṆICŪḌA (*looking at her, dismayed*): Queen, do not be afraid!

PADMĀVATĪ (*dubious*): Is it my husband? Who else could it be? Or am I beginning now to see my husband in every other man?

MAṆICŪḌA (*weeping*): I am the one you see. It is I! Truly I cause my kinsfolk much suffering!

GAUTAMA: O Queen, how could you even think it might be someone else? Why this is our dear friend Maṇicūḍa!

Padmāvatī looks at the two, and overcome by great distress faints in a swoon to the ground.

ŚABARAS: Hey you, come over here!

GAUTAMA (*lifting his cudgel*): Be on your way, you sons of slaves, you vile and wicked Śabaras. With this crooked cudgel, a cudgel like an angry snake, I'm going to smash in your heads.

MAṆICŪḌA: My friend, you must not talk that way!

16 "By doing a favor one cannot seal a friendship
as much as by forgiving a wrong."
This is the thought behind the notion
that all sentient beings forgiven in this manner
are induced to change their ways.

THE TWO ŚABARAS (*looking at each other*): He is exceedingly steadfast! How could he ever falter? For this reason we will now take our leave. By the power of his personality, this man has brought us to change our minds.

They act out in pantomime a state of fear and exit.

MAṆICŪḌA: O my Queen, how have you gotten into such a situation?

PADMĀVATĪ (*weeping*): You, my husband, and you are asking me about my fate?

GAUTAMA: O Queen, how is the Prince Padmottara?

PADMĀVATĪ (*looking up to the heavens*): Of what use is this tormenting question to me now, unfortunate woman that I am?

MAṆICŪḌA (*dismayed*): What about the boy?

PADMĀVATĪ: I wonder where my son Padmottara is now . . . ?

GAUTAMA: What are you saying, O Queen? Speak!!!

PADMĀVATĪ: I wonder what is happening to him . . . ?

GAUTAMA: O Queen, how is the Prince?

PADMĀVATĪ: Someone has taken him from me once again!

MAṆICŪḌA: With my son stolen away, I find myself once more in circumstances more than flesh and blood can bear. (*Weeping*) O woman so fraught and overflowing with insult and injury — I imagined a forest hermitage to be a bit different!

GAUTAMA (*weeping*): Alas, the insatiable God of Death has snatched him away! (*After this thought, continuing:*) O Queen, how did so sad and suffering a fate become your lot?

PADMĀVATĪ: It came to pass when I ventured forth from my hermitage to pick flowers.

MAṆICŪḌA: Queen, the great sage Marīci will be angry if he does not find you. Get up now! Be on your way and return to him!

GAUTAMA: Hardly has she escaped the captivity of the Śabaras and fallen into your hands, when you wish to send her back where she was before!

MAṆICŪḌA: What you say does not accord with the norms of the moral law!

PADMĀVATĪ (*weeping*): My husband, do you wish once again to drive me away?

MAṆICŪḌA: And do you then want to fling me into the abyss of sin? Behold:

17 If I should wish to take back something
which I previously had given away,
is that not like a dog that
in full public view
slurps up its own vomit?
Even though we lived together
for a very long time,
it is certain that we must separate
at some time to come.

And the Buddha has proclaimed the following:

18 All that is accumulated
is in time used up and consumed;
all who are exalted are hurled into the depths;
all that is united must separate in time;
all that is living finally must die.

Moreover, O Queen:

19 Separation is the nature of all things,
though long they may have been united.
Inescapably we are caught
by the God of Death in his noose,
and he opens wide his devouring mouth.
Immediate separation is far more desirable
even than joining in union,
if it occurs for the sake and good of the moral law.

PADMĀVATĪ: My husband, I will go where you have said. But though I want to depart, my feet refuse to carry out my will!

MAṆICŪḌA: Queen, morality dictates that you must follow my command! My friend, accompany the Queen to the domicile of the great sage!

GAUTAMA: Friend, I will do as you have said.

PADMĀVATĪ (*weeping*): O Gautama, wait just a moment. I would like to look upon my husband one more time. I have suffered the blows of fate, and there is little chance I will ever see him again. (*Looking at him full of affection*) My husband, give me one good last look as well! I will not lay eyes on you ever again.

MAṆICŪḌA: What is the use of looking at each other, my Queen? All that is united must one day in this manner go separate ways. Behold:

20 Thus do travelers who have journeyed
a portion of the way together,
later separate and go off again
in different directions,
despite their brief and temporary union.
This holds true as well
for members of the same family.

GAUTAMA: O friend, do not be unmerciful! Console the Queen!

MAṆICŪḌA (*weeping*): But how then should I console her?

21 *If I were told that*
we will meet again at some future time;
that your son Padmottara will some day
direct ministers and lead an army;
that I will once more lay my eyes upon
the parents-in-law of the Queen,
my very own parents,
in pure and radiant transfiguration;
and that people will speak of my subjects
as thriving and safe from threat:
then I would gladly console her!

A voice from the dressing room:

So shall it be!

All are amazed. Once more from the dressing room:

So shall it be!

GAUTAMA and PADMĀVATĪ:

22 He upon whom the Vidyādharas,
rushing over in their exaltation,
have rained down flowers from the heavens,
has become a creature radiant!

MAṆICŪḌA (*filled with shame*): Queen, should anyone chance by this place and see me in your presence, the rumor may spread that I have broken my promise.

PADMĀVATĪ (*weeping, showing him homage*): The gods will indeed look upon your person and judge your behavior! (*After saying this, she gazes at him one last time and sets out to leave the stage. The Vidūṣaka follows her.*)

MAṆICŪḌA (*watching them leave*):

23 I have given away as a gift a jewel of a wife,
and have attained all my earthly goals.
This crest-jewel has now become as useless as chaff.

O that some noble-hearted person might now appear bearing a request! (*As he thinks this aloud, a Brāhman enters*):

BRĀHMAN: Now, I am a supplicant! (*He approaches.*)

PADMĀVATĪ (*looking back*): Gautama, I believe this Brāhman wishes to ask something of you!

GAUTAMA: O Queen, he is a Brāhman. Since we Brāhmans never voluntarily give anything away, it is clear that he wants to ask something. Stay on, my Queen, hide here in the thicket and watch! I will return to them.

BRĀHMAN (*looking in his direction*): Why, it's King Maṇicūḍa!

24 The entire triple world is permeated
by the charisma of this single person,
as though he were the exalted lotus-born Brahma
at the threshold of a new world age.

(*Turning toward the King*) Hail to the King!

MAṆICŪḌA: Welcome, and sit down. (*When his right eye twitches auspiciously, he thinks to himself:*)

25 Since my right eye is twitching,
and everything is overflowing
with a bountiful radiance,
it is most certainly a great man,
possessed of a laudable clarity of mind,
who has appeared as a supplicant.

Great Brāhman, what is your request? Speak!

BRĀHMAN (*seemingly ashamed*): Indeed I have a very great wish!

MAṆICŪḌA (*joyously*): Enough of these airs and affectations! Everything that belongs to me is yours as well!

BRĀHMAN:

Friend of man, you who
bestow tranquility of mind,
and whose chief trait of character it is
to promote the benefit of others—
it is the crest-jewel upon your head that I desire.

GAUTAMA (*rushing over alarmed*): Hey there, Brāhman! You are lacking in even the most rudimentary sense of shame! Do you wish to ruin the bodily condition of my dear friend as well—and in such a painful and agonizing manner?

MAṆICŪḌA: Friend, you must not speak this way! Do you want to withhold from me the opportunity to perform a sacrifice?

27 This man is the donor,
and I am here the beggar!
Why, O friend, do you wish
to change this into its very opposite?
For me this is an excellent
vehicle to omniscience,
a vehicle which becomes
the cause for the nirvana
of all sentient beings.

Moreover:

28 If one compares the salutary properties
of a wishing-jewel with those of a supplicant,
then the supplicant emerges
as the better of the two:

For while a wishing-jewel provides one only
with worldly possessions,
through the action of a supplicant
one acquires all virtues.

O Brāhman, tear this crest-jewel from my head as you desire, and take it with you!

BRĀHMAN:

29 Who then would have the strength
to remove the crest-jewel of the King,
so very like the summit of Mt. Meru?

MAṆICŪḌA: Tear it out by smashing my skull with a stone! Behold:

30 The round of rebirths
for this egoless, ruined body,
so like a desiccated kadalī tree,
which is the symbol of fragility,
will come to an end
by having this body bring men joy and delight—
as a result of its usefulness for others.

GAUTAMA: Help! Help, O you gods of the forest. An evil and malevolent Brāhman wishes to kill my friend!

PADMĀVATĪ (*aghast*): Can one behold anything more harrowing than this? (*She rushes over.*)

BRĀHMAN (*filled with astonishment, to himself*): Are these the forest gods approaching?

PADMĀVATĪ: My husband, what is the meaning of this deed?

MAṆICŪḌA: My wish for a supplicant has now been fulfilled!

PADMĀVATĪ (*weeping*): Ha! My husband's wish has now been fulfilled? Why, it is the Brāhman's desire that has here been satisfied!

MAṆICŪḌA: Enough now of this excessive confusion of the spirit! Behold:

31 All living beings are tossed about
in the ocean of samsara by the waves of karma.
The exalted are hurled into the depths,
and those in the depths are revered by all.

BRĀHMAN: Since I too feel sympathy seeing this intensely compassionate soul, I now wish to leave the crest-jewel in its place.

PADMĀVATĪ: Thus do you strive to emulate Maṇicūḍa in your compassion!

GAUTAMA (*pleased*): Well said!

MAṆICŪḌA (*deeply dismayed*): O Brāhman, is it proper for you to act this way after having spoken so differently?

BRĀHMAN: Our country is being ravaged by the plague. This is why I wanted to take the crest-jewel and use its power to restore health to the people there.

MAṆICŪḌA (*distressed*): What was that, Brāhman? What did you just say?

BRĀHMAN: O King,

32 Villages and houses have become as though
ghastly cemeteries of death;
the decaying bodies, their limbs stretched stiff
in death's agony, look like piles of stacked wood.
Dogs and goblins have entered there,
even upon the highest mountains.
All this has come to pass
in the land of the Kurus!

MAṆICŪḌA: This grieves me. Is there then, O Brāhman, no way to reduce and alleviate the plague?

BRĀHMAN: To cause this "Black Death" to abate, the people there have sent me off with the charge of asking for the crest-jewel of the King.

MAṆICŪḌA (*extremely pleased*): Thus you are asking for my crest-jewel in order to render thereby a service unto other men! (*Saying this, he rips the jewel from his head.*)

33 Now that I have removed the crest-jewel,
a gem of vast proportions,
white as the moonbeams,
fastened at its base to my head,
and have brought it forth
and given it over to the Brāhman,
who with its agency will promote
the well-being of men,
may it put an end to the diseases
that plague all peaceable living creatures!

Saying this, he hands the jewel over to the Brāhman and faints in a swoon, in pantomime.)

PADMĀVATĪ (*weeping*): O my husband, mighty friend of the weak and defenseless, do you wish to abandon me here in my loneliness?

GAUTAMA: Save my dearest friend, this so affectionate friend of all sentient beings, O save him! The wishing-tree is being abandoned, and the ocean of generosity will dry up totally!

BRĀHMAN (*to himself*): What use is it for me to stay on here any longer? He is a man of noble character, and I wish only to fulfill his longing and desire. (*He walks about, then looks in a specific direction.*)

(*To himself*) Here comes a sage. Since I have committed a terrible sin, I will flee from here before he catches sight of me. (*Brāhman exits.*)

Enter the sage Marīci accompanied by Ratnāvalī.

SAGE (*to himself*):

34 Why do we hear the rumble of such loud thunder
at this unseasonable time?
Why is the whole earth trembling?
Why are even the winds so cold and raw, and
Why do the heavens themselves turn a whitish grey?
Why is the sun, across the breadth
of its entire surface,
being clutched by the moon,

the Lord of Planets, and so eclipsed?
Why now at this noon hour are all regions
wrapped in darkness?

It would appear that some unwanted sorrow has befallen the King. (*To Ratnāvalī*) Ratnāvalī, where has Padmāvatī gone?

RATNĀVALĪ: To the banks of the Mandākinī to pluck flowers.

SAGE: Let us hurry then to that place! (*While they walk, he indicates that he hears something.*) O, that sounds like someone weeping. I must most certainly hurry at once to that spot! (*They look about while continuing to walk.*)

RATNĀVALĪ (*weeping*): Exalted One, it is Padmāvatī who is sobbing so inconsolably. And there is Gautama also.

SAGE: There is someone else there as well!

RATNĀVALĪ (*looking in that direction*): O woe is me! It is King Maṇicūḍa — he is lying unconscious upon the ground!

SAGE: Woe is me! Unfortunate man that I am! The transitoriness of things is ever powerful!

35 He who always lived as a wishing-tree
for all sentient beings
now lies here unconscious.
Truly, happiness lasts but a short moment!

My daughter Padmāvatī, what has happened? You are weeping so bitterly!

GAUTAMA: Exalted One, just look!

SAGE: What has happened?

GAUTAMA: Exalted One, Maṇicūḍa has given away his crest-jewel!

SAGE: O you wishing-tree, you singular friend of all sentient beings!

PADMĀVATĪ (*embracing Ratnāvalī*): My dearest friend, come over here and look upon the end of his earthly being! O my son Padmottara, your father has left you also!

Enter Padmottara and Subāhu at the other side of stage.

PADMOTTARA: Here I am!

SUBĀHU:

36 I have found Padmāvatī here again
and have conquered King Duṣprasaha.
I left the city of Sāketa to seek out the King.
Is there anything else I can do for you?

PADMOTTARA: Honorable Prime Minister, I would like now to come face to face with my father and my mother.

SUBĀHU: Prince, so be it!

While they walk, Padmottara suddenly falls startled to the ground.

PADMOTTARA: Honorable One, something seems to have stung my foot!

Subāhu takes a quick look, ponders the situation, and then collapses in dread, falling to the ground.

SUBĀHU (*to himself*): That was definitely a snake. It just crawled into a crack in the ground and disappeared. The fulfillment of my wish now appears to be impossible — unless Padmottara rushes to the King and immediately seeks to counteract the effect of the poison with the rays emanating from the crest-jewel. (*Aloud*) Hurry up! Let's go look for your parents!

PADMOTTARA: My leg feels so numb and cool. It's falling asleep, and my body too is beginning to tremble.

SUBĀHU (*indicating that he hears something, to himself*): Here too we hear the sound of sobbing. (*Pondering to himself*) Is this not the weeping of the Queen? Why that is Ratnāvalī, and this person here is the exalted Marīci, is it not? (*In great consternation*) But why is everyone crying? (*Looking once again in that direction*) They are weeping, and the King continues to sleep. Oh how did the King's head get into such a sorry state? (*Looking more carefully*) O my great King, how did you get into such a plight?

37 Your eye has closed,
and now the world is without lustre.
The crest of your head looks empty and desolate
like a sunless sky.

(*Bowing down before the head of the Hero*) Not only has the King departed from this life, but now the Prince will also die, for the King has been deprived of the radiance of his crest-jewel.

PADMĀVATĪ (*embracing Ratnāvalī*): My son Padmottara, look one last time at your father — you will never see him again!

PADMOTTARA: Why is father lying there in that condition?

PADMĀVATĪ: Such is the special nature of his fate!

PADMOTTARA: Father, get up! Mother is still crying! (*He faints in a swoon, in pantomime.*)

PADMĀVATĪ and RATNĀVALĪ: O son, O Prince! O my little boy, will you now leave us too?

SUBĀHU: Alas, he has breathed his last! Woe is me! Now a blessed race of kings has been extinguished!

GAUTAMA: Padmottara, wake up!

SAGE (*astonished, looking in a specific direction*):

38 Now do the Vidyādharas send
a stream of sandal-water droplets
raining down upon his head.
They scatter from afar flowers
besprinkled with bees
as they fly through the skies.
The rivers flow gently by,
the waterdrops gleam and glisten
upon the deep Mandākinī,
and the holy red basil
here in the mountain gorges
intoxicates our senses.

All gaze upon this in great astonishment.

PADMĀVATĪ: The gods seemingly want to transport the body of my husband up into the world of the gods, that he might be venerated there. (*After saying this, she pays homage to the feet of the sage.*) O Exalted One, please grant in your mercy permission for me to go forth from here! (*Looking at Subāhu*) Make preparations for my pyre! These are my final instructions!

GAUTAMA: O Queen, tarry a moment! I too wish to follow after my dear friend, together with you!

SAGE: But why do you continue to weep? Do you not see

39 That his heart is beating strongly
and his eye is twitching;
that his mouth opens
like the blossom of a water-lotus;
that the hair upon his body
is beginning to tremble and his hand to move;
that his eyes once more
begin to show pity upon mankind?

GAUTAMA: O Queen, don't become agitated! My dear friend Maṇicūḍa might notice!

PADMĀVATĪ (*looking that way*): Miserable woman that I am, now I can breathe! (*Clasping Padmottara's hand*) My son, breathe freely, breathe a sigh of relief! Your father is alive!

RATNĀVALĪ: The King's retinue can again breathe freely!

The King recites again the verse beginning "Now that I have removed the crest-jewel . . ." [Verse 33]. Gradually his complexion takes on a fresh and glowing hue.

PADMĀVATĪ: O my husband, here is Prince Padmottara! Don't you want to hug and embrace him?

MAṆICŪḌA: Padmottara, come over here!

SUBĀHU: What can I say in this sad situation? My King, while I was resting along the way, Padmottara went on ahead and was bitten by the fangs of a snake, and is now unconscious.

MAṆICŪḌA (*astonished*): What is the meaning of this?

PADMĀVATĪ: Alas, did my son not see his father in time?

RATNĀVALĪ: O dearest friend, your most cherished desire has not been fulfilled!

GAUTAMA: O insatiable God of Death!

SUBĀHU: Where is the crest-jewel of the King?

GAUTAMA: He gave it to a Brāhman!

SUBĀHU: He was destroyed by a deception. This was most certainly a cunning trick of King Duṣprasaha. O King, how can you give away your crest-jewel so that your enemies might live?

MAṆICŪḌA: Even in times to come I will not regret this.

SAGE: How can you know that?

MAṆICŪḌA: Exalted One,

40 If I have never regretted my having given it away,
then now—by this act of truth, this *satyakriyā*,
and as a fruit of my compassionate character—
may a new crest-jewel sprout forth
for the benefit of all sentient beings,
a jewel of much greater potency and strength
than the one before!

After hearing these words, all act out in pantomime startled amazement, as though they had seen a flash of lightning. Padmottara rises.

SAGE: O, the character of this noble man is of perfect purity!

41 Now that a new crest-jewel has sprouted forth
upon the head of the ruler,
shining radiantly, as though emitting
thousands of sunbeams,
the darkness of poison
spread through the body of Padmottara
has been destroyed by its power,
and Padmottara once again opens his eyes,
like the blooming of a lotus blossom.

All express joyous surprise, in pantomime.

PADMĀVATĪ (*looking toward the King, embracing Padmottara*): His eyes have opened again!

GAUTAMA: My dear friend has revealed his magic power!

RATNĀVALĪ: To behold such a thing gives us great joy!

SUBĀHU: Prince, show your parents respect and veneration!

Padmottara places his palms together and shows his respect.

MAṆICŪḌA: May you ever and always be virtuous!

PADMOTTARA: May I become like my father!

SAGE: I now give you the Queen and Prince! May the King in his grace accept them!

MAṆICŪḌA: May it be as you have spoken!

All pantomime their great joy.

SAGE: Forgive me for having wronged you so!

MAṆICŪḌA: Why should there be any reason to forgive after an act of kindness?

From within the dressing room:

42 May you by your virtues fulfill
the most cherished desires
of all sentient beings!
May you in the desert of suffering
become the sea of sustenance;
a ladder upon which to ascend
the mountain of salvation.
May you become a ship leading
across the ocean of suffering,
and a source of illumination
in the unbearable darkness of ignorance!

May you become a place of refuge
for those in danger,
and a wishing-tree for those in need!

MAṆICŪḌA: What was that?

SAGE:

43 All the heavens are now filled with the gods—
Viṣṇu, Śiva, Brahmā,
Indra, and Soma at their head—
who dwell together with the other celestial hosts
in the heavenly palace.
These exalted ones, whose magical powers
wax even greater, and who flood the heavens with
the beauty of their white and yellow radiance,
have seemingly painted a mural
upon the vault of the sky.

Since your parents are present also, in a celestial vehicle, they most certainly desire to bless you, your son, and your consort.

The King and his retinue show their homage.

MAṆICŪḌA: Exalted One, tell me what I should do!

SAGE:

44 When you are absent, your subjects grieve—
return and protect them once again!
Indra himself has sent you this celestial vehicle
so you can quickly return to the city of Sāketa!

MAṆICŪḌA: May it come to pass as those on high have dictated!

All are extremely pleased. They act out in pantomime a journey in the celestial vehicle.

While they move about the stage, the King speaks:

MAṆICŪḌA: O, the celestial coach is very swift, for

45 The clouds, like a crowd of wanderers,
have disappeared, blown away by
the flapping wings of the geese.
The towering mountains rush
like a herd of rut-maddened elephants
directly into our midst.
The coach speeds like the discus
hurled by Indra, traveling northwards,
surrounded by the nimbus of the sun.

SAGE:

46 When King Duṣprasaha
and all the subjects of his empire
from the cities and countryside
see that you have put the hosts of Māra,
that foul pestilence, to flight,
and that the people are revived,
all will show you their homage.
Having flown past them and their country,
you now find yourself once again
in the city of Sāketa.

Tell me what further service I can do to please you?

MAṆICŪḌA: What more pleasant thing than this could there be?

47 *What else is there to complete,*
what else to undertake,
after I have once more beheld the faces
of Padmāvatī and my son, and dear Gautama,
who now have all journeyed here to this place;
and after I have witnessed my parents sitting
in a celestial coach, accompanied by hosts of gods;
and after the sorrow of my Prime Minister
and my subjects has entirely abated?

Nonetheless, there are still more pleasant things to do.

The Bharatavākya

48 May all living beings rejoice
in hearing the holy Dharma—
may it be for them the joy and delight
of a festival never-ending!
May the desires of the God of Death,
which have long waxed ever stronger,
be without fruit and of no avail!
May the radiance of the moon
(as well as that of Candragomin),
which supplies the subject
for the words and tales of holy sages,
and is cool and rich in blessings,
by its rain of nectar bring success!

Final Verse

49 May the actors, who have provided pleasure
long and great to the audience
through the truths of the author,
be granted a rich abundance of wealth,
and may they continue for many years to come
to please and delight the hearts of men!
May this *Lokānandanāṭaka*,
this drama offering joy for the world
in diverse and manifold ways,
which was composed by the Exalted One
who bears the name the "Dispassionate One,"
after he had discovered
in the person of Maṇicūḍa
an object of veneration,
continue to be presented on the stage!

After these words all exit.

End of Act Five

Colophon of the Sanskrit Manuscript

This is the instructive play Lokānanda, which treats the legend of Prince Mañicūḍa and was composed by the great teacher Candragomin.

Colophon of the Tibetan translation

Making use of the method of the great translators, the great pandit Kīrticandra and Grags-pa rgyal-mtshan from Yar-lungs prepared a most admirable translation of the play in the Nepalese city of Yambu (now Kathmandu).

Notes and Comments

Act One

Pre The prelude of any classical Indian drama consists of three parts:

the prayer or benediction (*nāndī*), in which the stage director invokes the tutelary god or goddess of the play, in this case the Buddha;

the first part of the prologue (*prastāvanā*), in which the stage director introduces the play and its author, and sometimes also the patron of the poet;

the second part of the prologue (*āmukha*), a kind of transitional passage, in which the stage director starts a dialogue with his wife, the dancer, which gradually and almost imperceptibly leads to the opening scene of the play.

I.2 The stanza contains a clear allusion to the four immeasurables or "infinitudes" (*apramāṇa*): "love" (Skt. *maitrī*, Tib. *byams pa*), "joy" (Skt. *muditā*, Tib. *dga' ba*), "compassion" (Skt. *karuṇā*, Tib. *snying rje*), and "equanimity" (Skt. *upekṣā*, Tib. *btang snyoms*). Hereby Candragomin indicates the theme of the whole play.

The scene alluded to in this stanza is the Buddha's enlightenment at the banks of the river Nairañjanā, close to present day Bodh Gaya. After they have unsuccessfully tried to disturb the Buddha's meditation, Māra's daughters address him ironically: "Why are you so imperturbable? Toward your wife Yaśodharā you showed quite a different kind of equanimity when you still led a married life! Why do you not now show this kind of equanimity toward us?"

I.3 This stanza describes the second attempt at disturbing the Buddha's final meditation before his enlightenment, when Māra's army stages a fierce attack on the Buddha in order to terrify him. The "ten powers" refer to the ten attributes of perfection traditionally ascribed to any Buddha or Arhat.

I.4 The Sanskrit title of the play, *Lokānanda,* contains a pun, because it can refer both to the play, "(the play that is) a joy for the world," and its hero Maṇicūḍa, "(the Bodhisattva who is) a joy for the world." This ambiguity is clearly felt in the original Sanskrit.

I.5 The expression "though he was unable to bear the burden of rule" seems to point to an incident in Candragomin's life in which he resigned from an official post. Such an incident is recorded in the work of the Tibetan historian Tāranātha (17th century), but that account may be based on this very passage.

I.6 In this stanza Candragomin alludes to his other literary and scientific compositions. The attributes "concise, abundantly clear, yet comprehensive in scope" are also mentioned in the beginning of some parts of Candragomin's famous grammar of the Sanskrit language.

I.6 Here the transitional portion of the prologue begins.

I.7 The stage director and his wife seem to talk about their own son but in fact they have already taken over the role of Maṇicūḍa's parents. They complain that Maṇicūḍa shows no interest in his royal duties but is attached to the life of an ascetic.

I.7 The miraculous event that heralded Maṇicūḍa's birth — the blossoming of all manner of things on the wishing tree (*kalpavṛkṣa* or *kalpataru*) of paradise — is described in some old versions of the Maṇicūḍa legend. Candragomin obviously presupposes acquaintance with this incident on the part of his audience.

I.8 First the stage director indirectly informs the audience about the happy end of the play ("By dint of his great merit he will attain the highest happiness and bliss."); then he invites his wife to undertake the conventional beginning of a Sanskrit drama: a song referring to one of the seasons.

I.9 The sentence "the blossoms of the *palāśa* tree gleam blood-red like meat quartered and minced" anticipates Maṇicūḍa's self-sacrifice to the demon in Act Four. "Crest-jewel" (*cūḍāmaṇi*) is the key word introducing the hero.

I.10 Note that the heavenly fairy, the Vidyādharī, is directly introduced by the stage director. In a similar manner characters appearing onstage will be introduced by those who are already on the stage.

I.12 Ratnāvalī's speech is unintentionally ambiguous. Most of the expressions used by her allow for two different interpretations. This kind of pun cannot fully be conveyed into another language. "Fire," "splendor," and "appearance" can be used in such a way that they may refer both to the moon and a human being. The terms *dharma*, meaning both "moral commandments" and "(astrological) laws," and *kalā*, meaning both "artistic skills" and "phases of the moon," lack a one-word equivalent in English, so the second meaning has been given in parentheses. The ambiguity of Ratnāvalī's speech is of course used by Candragomin to create the confusion that follows, which clearly depicts the emotional state of the two girls Mādhavī and Padmāvatī.

I.12 The dark spots in the moon are interpreted by Indian poets either as a gazelle or a hare; accordingly, the moon can be called "bearer of a gazelle (or hare)."

According to Indian mythology, Madana, the god of love, who is also called Kāma ("lust") or Anaṅga ("bodyless") lost his body when he tried to disturb the meditation of Śiva and the enraged god reduced him to ashes with a glance from his third eye. (page 11)

"Planetary wanderer through the heavens" refers to the Vidyādharī's ability to fly. (page 12)

The expression "unspeakable" contains a pun that cannot be fully retained in the English rendering. The Sanskrit word *avadya* usually means "faulty, blamable," but Mādhavī ambiguously uses it in its etymological meaning of "one who cannot be addressed." That his portrait cannot be addressed is of course not the fault of Maṇicūḍa. (page 13)

That nectar, the drink of the gods, may turn into poison is part of the old Hindu myth of the Churning of the Ocean (*samudramanthana*) at which occasion not only nectar (*amṛta*) but also the deadly poison Halāhala emerged. Śiva drank it and held it in his throat, thus saving all living beings from death. (page 14)

I.13 This stanza is a direct allusion to Padmāvatī's future motherhood.

I.15 The girls wrongly imagine that Bhavabhūti has overheard not only Padmāvatī's sobbing but also the dialogue preceding it.

I.17 This stanza uses numerous technical terms relating to the art of painting. Candragomin hereby displays his knowledge of this technical discipline. This is a common trait of Indian ornate poetry.

I.19 The expression "creator molding the fate of men" (the Tibetan translation is quite unclear here) might refer to Bhavabhūti's gift for prophecy.

I.20 The description of a peaceful scene at the end of an act is a common convention in an Indian drama.

I.21 The introduction of a concluding verse at the end of every act in which the author refers to himself approvingly is quite unusual in an Indian drama. Candragomin must already have been a celebrated and honored author to allow himself such an appraisal of his own person. One might suspect that the act-concluding stanzas are later additions from the pen of one of his admirers, but one fact that speaks against such an assumption is that his "Letter to a Disciple" also uses the word *candra* ("moon") in the first and last stanzas of the poem.

Act Two

Ent Another typical feature of the Indian drama is to connect the acts by short interludes (here, the entr'acte), which are classified into various types by the theoreticians. Leaving aside their subtle specifications, it may suffice to point to the fact that these interludes are a convenient means to advance the plot by summarizing events which have taken place in the meantime or to describe actions which by convention are not allowed to be shown on the stage. Usually it is the minor characters who figure in these interludes.

II.4 The jester Gautama points to the negative consequences that will occur if Maṇicūḍa, the last member of his royal family, fails to marry and beget a son. Contrary to the Buddhist ideal of extinction, the pious Hindu wishes to be kept alive in the world of the gods even after his death by the offerings made to him by his (male) children and their offspring. These offerings, and especially the water offered at these occasions, should never cease to flow.

II.6 From the words uttered by Maṇicūḍa in this stanza, Ratnāvalī immediately concludes that Padmāvatī's wish to marry the prince cannot be fulfilled and that she will die of a broken heart. (page 28)

II.11 Ratnāvalī is misled by the maidservant's words; she thinks Maṇicūḍa is married to a different girl, which again means the end of Padmāvatī's hopes. (page 30)

II.17 This stanza contains a nice pun based on the Sanskrit word *sneha*, which means both "love" and "oil." "Love" is the reason human beings are reborn again and again, just as a lamp continues to burn as long as there is a supply of oil. In order to attain nirvana it is therefore necessary to abandon such love.

II.20 The phrase "darkness of delusion" attempts to render into English the two meanings of Sanskrit *moha*: "delusion," resulting from the pleasures of the senses, and "fainting," resulting from a strong poison.

II.25 The expression "granting a wish" is somewhat awkward in the context of the dialogue. "Purposeful action" is another possible translation of the hypothetical Sanskrit original *arthakriyā*. Even better would be "fruitful act," which presupposes Sanskrit *arthakarman*. Without the Sanskrit available it is rather difficult to ascertain precisely the meaning of the whole passage. (page 38)

II.26 "Maidens of poison" (*viṣakanyā*) are girls who intend to kill their bridegrooms by dripping poisoned sweat while walking around the nuptial fire. (page 39)

II.29 Gautama's words are meant to depict the greediness of the jester, who can think of nothing but his food.

II.30 The conversation between Gautama, Maṇicūḍa and Ratnāvalī is meant to present humorously Gautama's ignorance of the basic facts of astronomy, in contrast with Maṇicūḍa's experience in all branches of art and science. Much of the humor contained in the original text seems to have been lost in the course of translation.

II.31 The "Seven Rishis" or "Seven Seers" is the Indian name for the constellation of the Great Bear (Ursa Major). According to the Mahābhārata, they are Marīci, Atri, Angiras, Pulaha, Kratu, Pulastya, and Vasiṣṭha.

II.33 It is not quite clear what is meant by the expression "this place." Stanzas III.23 and V.49 suggest that Candragomin has in mind the stage on which Buddhist plays are performed.

Act Three

III.1 Kāma, the god of love, is said to have five arrows made of flowers.

III.3 A "wishing flower" is a metaphor for an object that symbolizes the fulfillment of a wish — in this case it is, of course, Padmāvatī.

III.4 The nectar Maṇicūḍa pours down comes from his crest jewel. It has a magical healing power. This first hint of the jewel's effect prefigures the role the jewel will play at the end of Act Five.

III.8 Flowers are usually offered only to gods. For that reason it is customary for human beings to remove a flower garland immediately after it has been given. (page 58)

III.13 Bhavabhūti points to the power of the gods and sages to utter dangerous curses against those who violate the rules of good conduct or otherwise cause their anger. Cf. also stanza III.16.

III.18 In the añjali gesture the palms of both hands are joined, leaving a cavity between them.

III.19 "The master of your life" means "your beloved."

III.19 Maṇicūḍa's pointing to the respect and homage he owes his parents is of course an evasion meaning: "I do not have the right to decide this matter without prior consultation with my parents." (page 65)

The "cloud of your hand" refers to the Indian custom in which at the wedding ceremony the bridegroom pours water from his hand into his bride's while reciting a blessing. (page 66)

III.22 This stanza contains the description of a peaceful evening scene. Compare the description of noon in I.20.

Act Four

Ent Like Act Two, Act Four begins with an interlude the purpose of which is to inform the spectators what has happened during the intervening period of time.

The phrase "carrying out the command of your father" (page 75) can be understood only by those who are familiar with the classical version of the Maṇicūḍa legend. There Bhavabhūti, Padmāvatī's foster father, gives her away to Maṇicūḍa on the condition that he perform the *nirargaḍa* sacrifice. For a summary of this version of the story, see the Introduction.

Mādhavi's innocent invitation "Become as before the ornament in the ascetic's abode"—meaning "Please return to the place of your former family"—anticipates Padmāvatī's sorrowful experience in being ordered to leave Maṇicūḍa and stay in the ascetic Marīci's hermitage. Mauñja somehow feels the negative effect of Mādhavī's words and therefore blames her.

Subāhu's words "five years ago" (page 76) indicate that another five years have elapsed following the dialogue in the interlude, in which the audience was informed of the birth of Padmottara. This is in harmony with Padmottara appearing on stage as a young boy, not as a newborn baby, later in this act. The Tibetan text, however, is not quite clear in this matter, as there is a variant reading which omits the number five.

IV.2 The god Indra received his epithet Śatakratu ("[characterized by] one hundred sacrifices") because it was thought that the making of one hundred horse-sacrifices would elevate the one carrying them out to the rank of

Indra. Since Maṇicūḍa has made a similar number of sacrifices having the same worth, he too can be called a god.

IV.6 Greed or craving is a central element in the nexus of conditioned origination, one of the basic elements of the Buddha's teaching. It leads to rebirth and to the wrong notion of an ego.

IV.7 The twitching of the king's left eye presages that something evil will happen to him. This is a common device in the Indian drama. *Ā śrauṣaṭ* is an old Vedic formula used at sacrifices.

IV.13 This formula can also be found in the oldest Indian religious texts.

IV.22 This stanza presents an intricate relationship between the temper of a person and the effect it has on the taste of his flesh. According to Indian medicine there are six basic tastes, all of which are mentioned in this stanza: bitter, burning, astringent, sour, pungent, and sweet. It is not clear on which medical authority Candragomin relies. This is again an intentional display of Candragomin's erudition. In addition, the relationship between temper and taste has an important dramaturgic function: The Rākṣasa "proves" that because of this relationship he can accept only the flesh of Maṇicūḍa.

IV.22 The Rākṣasa is a "friend who fosters (Maṇicūḍa's) salvation" (*kalyāṇamitra*) because he offers him an opportunity to accumulate merit of the highest order. (page 88)

IV.23 According to Indian cosmology the earth is a disk encircled by an ocean. Hence "girded by the ocean" is a common epithet of the goddess of earth.

IV.23 "Destroyer of the (three) cities" is one of Indra's epithets because he is credited with the destruction of Tripura, the "Triple City" of the demons called Asuras.

IV.36 This stanza anticipates the situation in which Maṇicūḍa will be found in the first part of Act Five (stanzas 7 and 8).

Act Five

V.1 The stanza contains an enumeration of all those things which are white or — according to the conventions of Indian poetry — symbolize the color white: fame, the splendor of certain jewels and garments, tranquility, a smile (because of the whiteness of the teeth), nectar, sandalwood, and the beams of the moon.

V.3 It is remarkable that Candragomin here invents an honorable motive for Marīci's demanding Padmāvatī from Maṇicūḍa. This motive is absent in the original legend. This stanza is the fulfillment of Mādhavī's prophetic words in the interlude preceding Act Four.

V.4 The exact meaning and function of the two sentences following this stanza is not quite clear.

V.7-8 A description of the situation anticipated in IV.36

V.10 Here in much abbreviated form the four classical stages of meditation are described. In the Pali Text Society Dictionary they are summarized as follows:

1) The mystic, with his mind free from sensuous and worldly ideas, concentrates his thoughts upon some special subject (for instance the impermanence of all things). This he thinks out by attention to the facts and by reasoning.

2) Uplifted beyond attention and reasoning, he experiences joy and ease both of body and mind.

3) The bliss passes away, and he becomes suffused with a sense of ease, and

4) he becomes aware of pure lucidity of mind and equanimity of heart.

V.12 The term "non-duality" points to the basic tenets of Mahāyāna philosophy, as developed in the Sūtras on the Perfection of Wisdom and the works of Nāgārjuna.

V.14 This is again a reference to a scientific treatment of the differences between male and female voices.

V.18 This is an old canonical verse the Sanskrit original of which is still available:

sarve kṣayāntā nicayāḥ patanāntāḥ samucchrayāḥ ||
saṁyogā viprayogāntā maraṇāntaṁ hi jīvitam ||

V.21 Maṇicūḍa outlines a number of specific conditions, the fulfillment of which is promised to the attentive spectator by the voice from the dressing room, although this seems well-nigh impossible under the prevailing circumstances.

V.24 Again the twitching of the king's eye presages something auspicious about to happen to him.

V.40 The belief in the effect of an "act of truth" (*satyakriyā*) is based on the assumption of the all-pervading, overwhelming power of truth. If and only if an utterance is absolutely true, then the consequences connected with it by the speaker will inevitably take place. A *satyakriyā* is a powerful but at the same time very dangerous means, as it might turn against the speaker.

V.47 This is the confirmation that the conditions put forward in V.21 have all been fulfilled.

V.47 This is the stereotyped question at the end of an Indian drama announcing the so-called *Bharatavākya*.

V.48 This final blessing at the end of the play is called *Bharatavākya* by the theoreticians. The stanza is identical with the concluding stanza of Candragomin's "Letter to the Disciple." Candragomin refers to himself by way of a pun containing the word "moon" (*candra*).

V.49 While the *Bharatavākya* is part of the drama, this second concluding stanza stands outside it, as do the concluding stanzas at the end of Acts One through Four. Here Candragomin clearly refers to himself by the expression "dispassionate one" (*vītarāga*), which is usually reserved for Bodhisattvas.

Glossary

ANAṄGA One of Māra's names; *see* Māra

APARĀJITĀ "The Invincible One"; name of a minor female Buddhist deity

AŚOKA Name of a tree (*Jonesia Asoka Roxb.*) that bears red flowers

BAKULA Name of a tree (*Mimusops Elengi*)

BRAHMĀ The Indian creator god

CAKRAVĀḌA (also spelled Cakravāla) The nine mythical mountain ranges encircling the earth with Mount Meru at the center

CANDRADĀDA Another name for Candragomin, author of the Lokānanda

DEVADĀRU Name of an Indian pine tree (*Pinus deodora*)

GUGGULU A particularly fragrant gum resin; *bdellium*

HIMAVANT "Snow-covered"; a name for the Himālayas

INDRA The chief of the gods in the heaven of the thirty-three gods

JĀTUKARṆA Name of an old Indian clan

JINA "The Victorious One"; one of the Buddha's names

KADALĪ The plantain tree (*Musa sapientium*), the symbol of essencelessness and fragility

KAUŚIKA An epithet of the god Indra

KINNARĪ A female Kinnara: mythical beings said to be particularly gifted for music

KURU Name of a people and the country occupied by them, to the north of present day Delhi

LAKṢMĪ The goddess of fertility, prosperity and abundance; the spouse of Viṣṇu

MADANA The god of love; *see also* Māra

MĀDHAVĪ The spring creeper, with white fragrant flowers

MADHŪKA Name of a tree, sometimes identified with the Aśoka tree

MĀLATĪ A kind of jasmine (with white fragrant flowers)

MALAYA The name of the mountain range on the western coast of India

MĀNASA Name of the sacred lake close to Mt. Kailāśa; also called Mānasarovar

MĀRA The Buddha's opponent, ruler over samsara; known also as Kāma, Madana, and Anaṅga

MANDĀKINĪ A name of the celestial river Gaṅgā (Ganges)

MERU Name of the mythical golden mountain which forms the central point of the universe

NĀGA Semi-divine, serpent-like beings who live beneath the earth

NĀGAKESARA A flower (*Mesua Roxburghii*)

NANDANA Name of the heavenly grove of the gods

NIRARGAḌA Literally "unbarred, unbolted, unrestrained"; name of a particular Buddhist sacrifice, in practice meaning unlimited donations to supplicants

PĀRIJĀTA Name of a mountain (found only in Buddhist literature)

PALĀŚA Name of an Indian tree (*Butea frondosa*) with dark red blossoms

PARIJĀTAKA The Indian coral tree (*Erythrina Indica*), said to be one of the five trees produced at the Churning of the Ocean and to grow in Indra's paradise

RĀKṢASA The general name for a class of malevolent spirits

ŚABARA Name of tribal peoples who live in the mountains

SĀKETA Name of an old Indian city, present day Oudh

ŚALMALĪ The silk-cotton tree (*Salmalia malabarica*)

SAMSARA The endless circle of continuous rebirths that continues until final extinction (nirvana) is reached; often compared to an ocean

SANTĀNA One of the five trees of Indra's paradise

SARASVATĪ The Indian goddess of learning and fine arts

ŚATAKRATU An epithet of god Indra, short for "He whose rank can be won by a hundred (horse-)sacrifices"

ŚEṢA "Remainder," also called Ananta ("Endless"): name of the thousand-headed King of the Nāgas, who bears the earth on his head

SOMA The lord of stars and planets, the moon-god

SVAYAṀBHŪ "Self-Born"; an epithet of the Buddha

TAMĀLA Name of a tree with very dark bark (*Xanthochymus pictorius*)

TĀRĀ Name of the popular and powerful female Buddhist Bodhisattva (literally, "the Savioress"), whose pious devotee Candragomin was said to be

TATHĀGATA "Thus Gone"; an epithet of the Buddha

VĀSUKI One of the mythical kings of the serpents (*nāga*) whose crest is adorned with precious jewels

VICULA The name of a plant (*Vangueria spinosa*) that is attested only in the dictionaries, not in any text; perhaps only an erroneous spelling of Nicula, a better known tree (*Barringtonia acutangula*)

VIDYĀDHARA The male counterpart of a Vidyādharī

VIDYĀDHARĪ A female Vidyādhara, "Bearer of Wisdom"; a beneficent aerial being of great beauty

VIṢṆU One of the three important gods of later Hinduism; the preserver of the universe and the embodiment of goodness and mercy

YAMA The god of death, who bears a black club

YAŚODHARĀ "Bearer of Glory"; name of the Buddha's wife when he was a prince in his final life

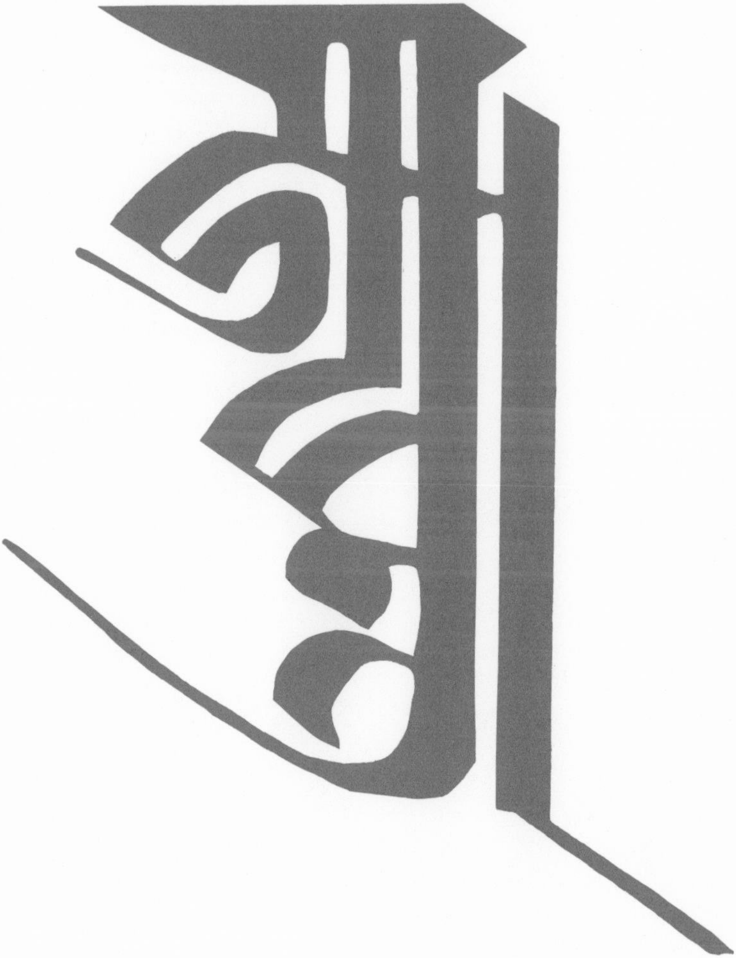

The symbol in ancient Lantsa script on the preceding page spells the Sanskrit word *Jayantu.* It signifies victory and expresses the wish that all people be truly free.